SENECA COUNTY AND THE CIVIL WAR

Seneca County and the Civil War

Walter Gable

The History Press

Published by The History Press
Charleston, SC 29403
www.historypress.net

First published 2014

Manufactured in the United States

ISBN 978.1.62619.633.9

Library of Congress CIP data applied for.

This book is dedicated to the memory of my great-grandfather John Loudebank Hoster.

John Loudebank Hoster
(July 15, 1842–October 30, 1930).

CONTENTS

ACKNOWLEDGEMENTS

Many people have greatly assisted me in making this book happen. Two of these are Carolyn Zogg and Naomi Brewer, fellow local historians who have become my close friends. They have been extremely helpful with proofreading draft chapters and preparing the book's index. Everyone should have two friends as dear as these two.

Bruce Lyon, my current office volunteer, deserves special mention. His assistance has made it possible for me to devote quality time to actual writing.

William Sebring, historian for the town of Romulus and hardworking member of the Sons of the American Revolution and the Sons of Union Veterans, has been a faithful mentor for this book.

Whitney Tarella Landis, commissioning editor for The History Press, has been just wonderful. Her guidance and support have been greatly appreciated.

The late Betty Auten, a former Seneca County Historian, spent the last several decades of her life gathering information on various soldiers from Seneca County, New York, who served in the Civil War. Her materials have been a wonderful information base for this book.

The Seneca County Board of Supervisors and several members of the county staff have been instrumental in making my work as the Seneca County Historian possible and so enjoyable. Their support is greatly appreciated.

The late Ethel M. Buckley, my high school history teacher, instilled in me a great love of history. At least one of her local history anecdotes is the basis of one of the chapters in this book.

Roberta Halden, as the historian for the former village of Seneca Falls, spent years compiling year-by-year notebooks of newspaper articles from various Seneca Falls newspapers. These notebooks are at the Seneca Falls Library and have been of tremendous help in the research for this book.

I thank the late Dale Theetge; his wife, Diane; and Jim Hughes for their help in providing one of my first major tasks as Seneca County Historian in early September 2003—lining up individuals to be interviewed by a freelance writer preparing a program on the Scythe Tree for the public radio station in Rochester. I also thank Wayne Mahood for his expertise in helping with the content for my first article on the story of the Scythe Tree.

INTRODUCTION

As the Seneca County Historian for the past ten years, I have continued to be amazed at how much "history" Seneca County has, especially given that U.S. census data for 2010 lists the county's population as 35,253. It is in Seneca County that we have the birth of the women's rights movement in 1848, the organization of the Latter Day Saints Church in 1830 and the world's largest herd of all-white white-tailed deer. Those events are not the subject of this book. The first part of this book tells about the many companies in which Seneca County men volunteered to serve and the interesting stories of several of these soldiers. One of these stories tells about William Cross and five of his sons who all served in the War. Three Seneca County men received the Medal of Honor. One chapter uses as much as possible the actual wording of John Loudebank Hoster, my great-grandfather, from daily journal entries for his entire wartime service, including his time as a prisoner at Andersonville, Georgia, and Florence, South Carolina. In April 2013, my brother Wayne and I visited the Andersonville and Florence sites to get a better grasp of how horribly traumatic his prison camp experiences must have been. Hoster's detailed information has been extensively used by historical scholars.

The second part of the book tells about what was happening in Seneca County during the war years. Farmers enjoyed some of their greatest prosperity as wheat prices soared. Following the war, many of these farmers built grand new homes with their wartime profits. Industries such as the Seneca Knitting Mill were expanding their productive capacity to keep

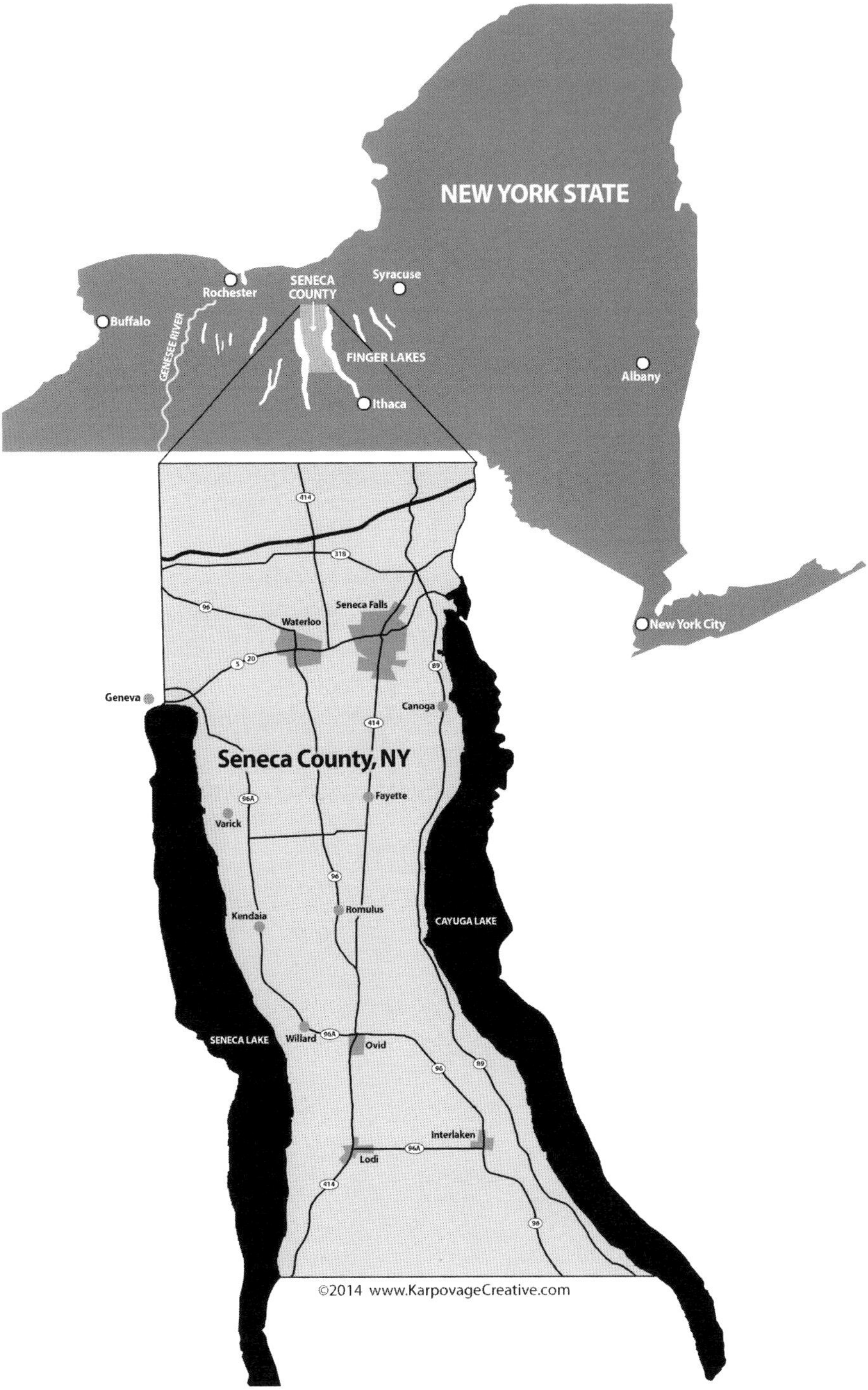
NEW YORK STATE
Rochester
SENECA COUNTY
Syracuse
Buffalo
GENESEE RIVER
FINGER LAKES
Albany
Ithaca
New York City
Seneca Falls
Waterloo
Geneva
Canoga
Seneca County, NY
Fayette
Varick
Romulus
Kendaia
CAYUGA LAKE
SENECA LAKE
Willard
Ovid
Interlaken
Lodi
©2014 www.KarpovageCreative.com

Above: Logo developed for Waterloo's 1966 centennial celebration of Memorial Day. *Waterloo Historical Society*.

Opposite: Seneca County is located in the heart of the Finger Lakes region. *Michael Karpovage of Karpovage Creative Inc.*

up with the military's demand for socks and long underwear. In the latter years of the war, the county and town governments continued to raise their bounties to get men to enlist to fill recruitment quotas.

The third part of the book describes how Seneca County residents have continued to preserve the legacy of the many county men who served in the Civil War. Waterloo is recognized as the official birthplace of Memorial Day because of events that took place in that community in 1865 and 1866. The Scythe Tree story began with James Wyman Johnson, who hung his scythe in a tree near the kitchen door and went off to serve in the war. There are five major Civil War monuments or memorials in the county, each with its own unique qualities. Many Civil War veterans joined one of the local Grand Army of the Republic (GAR) posts. As the Union veterans dwindled in numbers, these GAR posts were replaced by the Sons of Union Veterans and the Daughters of Union Veterans of the Civil War.

The year 2014 is a most appropriate year for the publication of this book because it marks the 100th anniversary of one event and the 150th anniversary of another. 2014 is the 100th anniversary of the chartering of the Caywood Camp, Sons of Union Veterans (SUV). Located in Ovid, the Caywood Camp is the only SUV camp in Seneca County. The Sons of Union Veterans is a fraternal organization dedicated to preserving the history and legacy of heroes who fought and worked to save the Union. It was 150 years ago that John L. Hoster was captured and spent four months in the Andersonville prison. Meanwhile, many soldiers were killed or wounded in the battles of the final year of the Civil War.

The book has been written as part of my work as the Seneca County Historian. Virtually all of the proceeds that I obtain from sales of this book will be going to three Seneca County–based organizations that are playing major roles in keeping alive Seneca County's Civil War history. These organizations are the National Memorial Day Museum, the Caywood Camp of the Sons of Union Veterans and the Mary Gahan Tent of the Daughters of the Union Veterans. My work in preparing this book has given me a much greater understanding of and appreciation for the important work of these groups.

Part I
ANSWERING THE CALL: THOSE WHO VOLUNTEERED

I appeal to all loyal citizens to favor, facilitate, and aid this effort to maintain the honor, the integrity, and the existence of our National Union, and the perpetuity of popular government.

—*President Abraham Lincoln, A Proclamation, April 15, 1861*

Chapter 1

INITIAL REACTION TO THE OUTBREAK OF THE CIVIL WAR

Following the election of Abraham Lincoln as president in November 1860, seven Southern states seceded from the Union before Lincoln was inaugurated on Mach 4, 1861. While it was common in the North to blame the Southern states for this secession, there was at least some strong anti-Republican sentiment that was placing the blame on this new Republican Party. A January 5, 1861 article in a pro-Democrat newspaper in Seneca Falls is an example of this sentiment:

> *The threatening aspect of our political affairs is well calculated to alarm the most conservative…The leaders of the* [Republican] *party have declared, over and over again, that there was an "irrepressible conflict" going on; that a "house divided against itself cannot stand;" that this government, which was formed in the spirit of compromise, and which has conferred so many blessings upon mankind, was a "failure;" that the States must all be devoted to freedom or slavery…For the first time in the history of the Republic, a sectional party has succeeded in electing a President.*
>
> *Its election has brought the country to the verge of revolution and civil war. Already the disintegration of the Republic has commenced, and the representatives of the party responsible for this state of things refuse to abate one iota of their fanaticism to save the Union. Their* [sic] *is no safety for the Southern States, nor protection to their interests, if the more radical doctrines and views enunciated by the Republican party are carried into effect under the administration of Abraham Lincoln.*[1]

The Civil War began in April 1861 with a quick succession of events. U.S. military forces holding Fort Sumter in the Charleston, South Carolina harbor entrance surrendered on Sunday, April 14, 1861. The *Seneca County Courier* newspaper reported the impact of this incident as follows:

> *Fort Sumter has fallen, and the first battle has been won by the Secessionists. It is a humiliating defeat for the proud American Nation; but there is compensation in the effect it has had upon the public mind. The fire that burned out and suffocated Anderson and his men has fused and mingled into one solid mass the divided elements of opinion… Henceforth there will be but one party at the North, and the Union men of the Border States will know that their hands are to be strengthened and their rights protected.*[2]

On Monday, April 15, President Lincoln called for seventy-five thousand volunteers to suppress the rebellion of the seven seceding states that called themselves the Confederacy. Lincoln's call was followed by the secession of four more states. Like virtually all counties, Seneca County residents very quickly responded to Lincoln's call for volunteers for the Union army. The Everts 1876 *History of Seneca County, New York* described the reaction as follows:

> *Americans are proud of the Republic, and their valor on land and sea has attested to their patriotic devotion. Conscious of their own loyalty, the yeomanry of New York looked calmly upon the secession of States and the cumulation* [sic] *of rebellious forces until, like a thunderbolt, fell the tidings of Fort Sumter bombarded and surrendered. Then the people forgot all but the peril of the land, and all over the North thousands rushed to arms…All over Seneca County the noble fervor spread, and from Seneca Falls, Waterloo and Ovid, companies of her choice young men went forth to battle.*

Patriotic Fervor in Seneca Falls

James E. Ashcroft, a twenty-one-year-old Seneca Falls dentist, was the captain of a well-drilled Zouave company. Foreseeing war, Captain Ashcroft, as early as November 1860, had unsuccessfully offered the service of his company to the New York governor. Following the fall of Fort Sumter on Sunday, April 14, 1861, Ashcroft quickly moved to organize a company of Seneca Falls volunteers. By Thursday, April 18, he had secured thirty-three enlistees to serve in a company. The company, which officially became Company C of the Nineteenth New York Volunteers, was composed of young men from eighteen to twenty-five years of age. Among them were two sons of Henry B. and Elizabeth Cady Stanton. Mrs. Stanton expressed her regret that her two younger sons were not old enough to enlist also. On April 27, 1861, this company departed Seneca Falls for Elmira "amid the plaudits of thousands" and accompanied by the Seneca Falls Cornet Band. They arrived in Elmira by 11:00 p.m. A rendezvous camp for upstate New York military units was being established there as quickly as possible, but it was not ready when these Seneca Falls men arrived. They were assigned to quarters in the Old Barrel Factory. They were issued soldiers' rations and straw and blankets in place of feather beds and white sheets. On June 6, the various companies of the Nineteenth New York Volunteers left for service in the area of Washington, D.C.

Seneca Falls contributed $3,000 toward the $23,277,000 that various states and communities gave as "Patriotic Contributions" to the U.S. government following the fall of Fort Sumter and prior to May 7, 1861. Seneca Falls was the only Seneca County community listed as making a donation. Neighboring communities such as Auburn, Canandaigua, Ithaca, Oswego and Syracuse also contributed. New York State donated $3,000,000 and New York City $2,173,000.[3]

The *Courier* newspaper of Seneca Falls expressed its patriotism in another way—by changing its masthead to include a large flag symbol and using the words "Union" and "Constitution." In late May 1861, the *Seneca Falls Reveille* characterized Seneca Falls as "a patriotic village":

> *Ours is emphatically a patriotic village. We have organized three full volunteer companies and sent them to the rendezvous at Elmira. About twenty of our young men enlisted in one of the Auburn companies, making the number of volunteers from this place about 260, and that too from a village of 5,000 inhabitants. If the rest of the State had done as well as our village there would now be over two hundred thousand volunteers mustered into service and ready to march to the protection of our country's Flag.*[4]

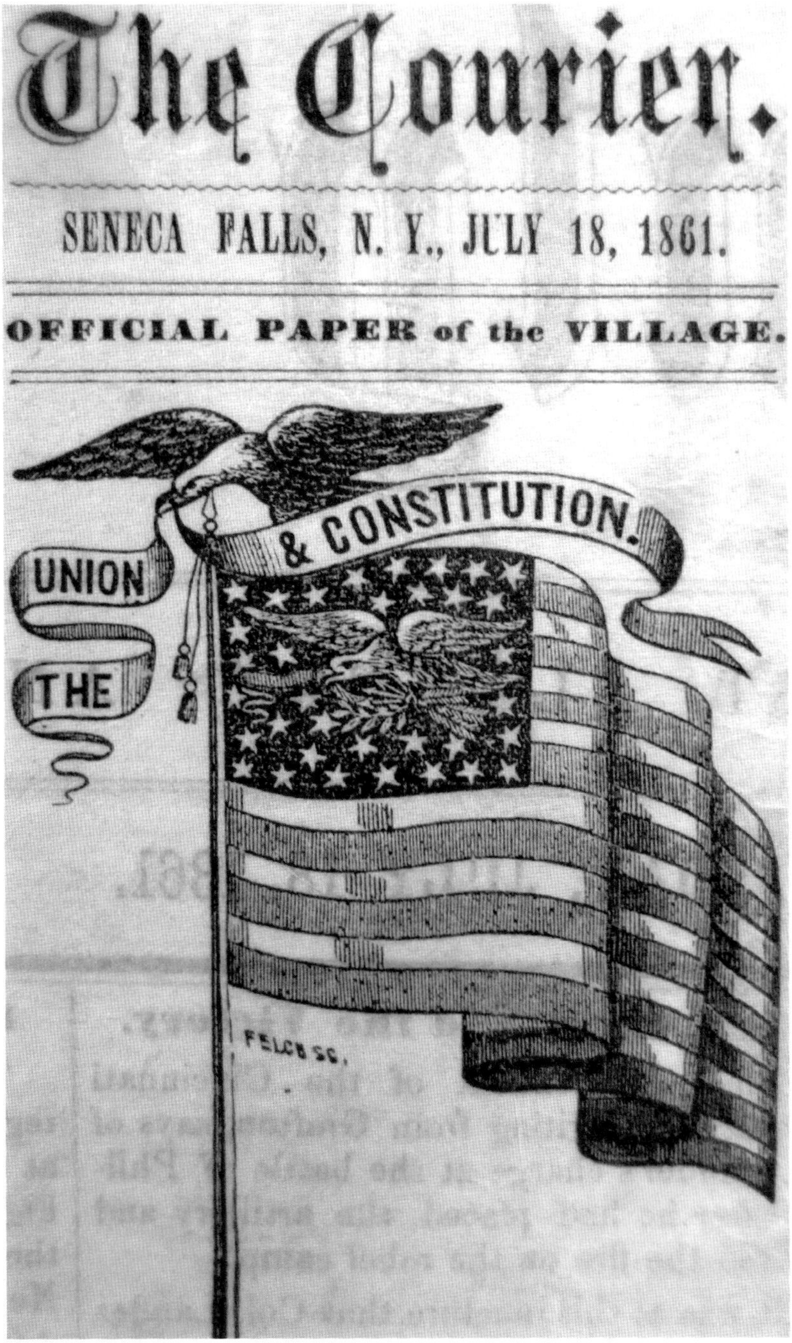

Patriotic new masthead for the *Seneca Falls Courier* following the outbreak of the Civil War. *Roberta Halden.*

For years in the greater Seneca Falls community, there had been a Volunteer Relief Committee, composed largely of upper middle-class businessmen and clergy, that provided assistance to families in need. This committee felt rather overwhelmed by the sudden need to provide aid to the approximately fifty families whose patriarchs had left for military service. On May 28, 1861, this committee put a notice in the local newspapers. The notice asked "the liberal and patriotic citizens of Seneca Falls and the surrounding country to subscribe liberally to the Volunteer Relief Subscription which…is necessary for the support of the families left in the care of the Committee."[5]

Later that summer, the Seneca Falls Union Agricultural Society decided that its annual fair proceeds would go to the "benefit of sick and wounded soldiers." Ladies of the community had to take on the responsibility of the actual planning of these fairs. One newspaper said that the 1862 fair would "undoubtedly far surpass anything of the kind which has ever taken place in the county" because it would be "under the direction of Ladies, who never fail when they undertake a public enterprise."[6]

Patriotic Fervor in Ovid

On Saturday, April 20, 1861, the first war meeting was held at the Ovid Court-House. The *Ovid Bee* reported that "all ages and classes were represented; political distinctions were entirely annihilated" in this massive gathering to organize a local company of volunteers. A resolution that was adopted contained a clause that stated, "…in view of all the facts and circumstances that now surround us, no man having the blood of an American citizen running through his veins can remain passive or neutral but is most imperitively [*sic*] called upon to define his position and array himself with those who stand pledged to support the Constitution and the Laws, and maintain the dignity and honor of the American flag." The *Ovid Bee* reported on May 1 that "public opinion has been so aroused and feelings enlisted with such just cause that all men loin for the Union and enforcement of the laws. The stars and stripes float from numerous points—the movements of our gallant volunteers, the shrill fife and roll of the drum, and the earnest conversations indicate the spirit and intensity of the war feeling in our

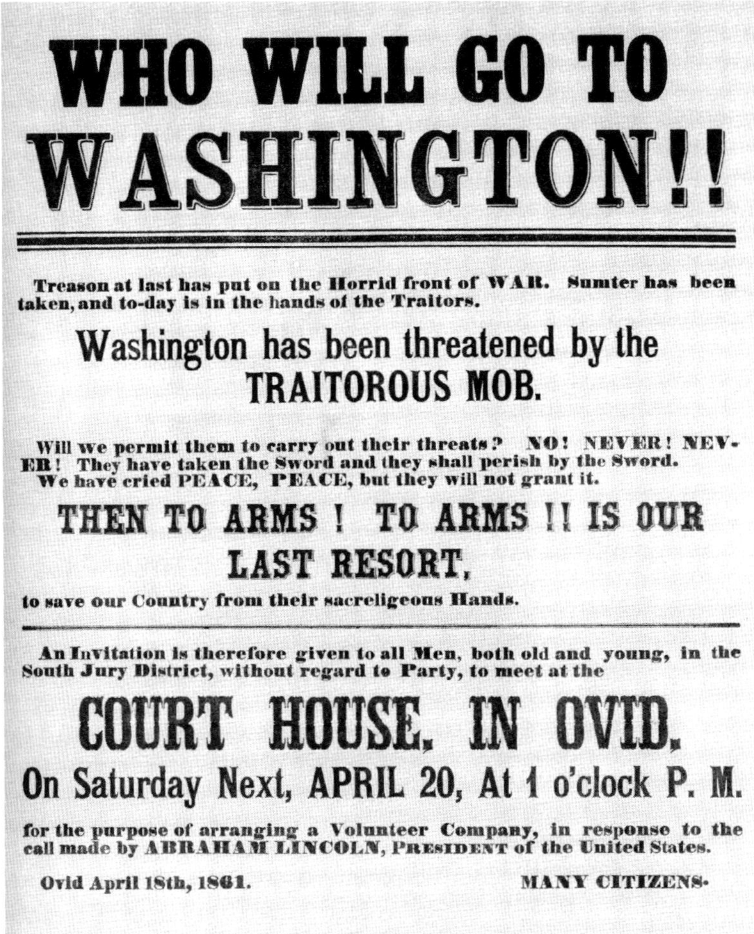

WHO WILL GO TO
WASHINGTON!!

Treason at last has put on the Horrid front of WAR. Sumter has been taken, and to-day is in the hands of the Traitors.

Washington has been threatened by the
TRAITOROUS MOB.

Will we permit them to carry out their threats? NO! NEVER! NEVER! They have taken the Sword and they shall perish by the Sword. We have cried PEACE, PEACE, but they will not grant it.

THEN TO ARMS! TO ARMS!! IS OUR
LAST RESORT,

to save our Country from their sacreligeous Hands.

An Invitation is therefore given to all Men, both old and young, in the South Jury District, without regard to Party, to meet at the

COURT HOUSE, IN OVID,

On Saturday Next, APRIL 20, At 1 o'clock P. M.

for the purpose of arranging a Volunteer Company, in response to the call made by ABRAHAM LINCOLN, President of the United States.

Ovid April 18th, 1861. MANY CITIZENS.

Poster urging Ovid area residents to attend an April 20, 1861 recruitment meeting. *Wayne Morrison.*

midst." According to Morrison's *History of Ovid, Seneca County, N.Y.*, the company consisted of sixty men, with Thaddeus Bodine as captain and David G. Caywood as lieutenant. On Saturday, May 11, these Ovid volunteers left for Elmira. By mid-July, they were on duty at Camp Granger in Washington, D.C.

Patriotic Fervor in Waterloo

Patriotic fervor was strong in Waterloo as well. What became known as Company C of the Thirty-third Regiment began as eighty-six men who were sworn into service at Waterloo on April 26, 1861. They were first known as the Wright Guards, organized by Captain John F. Aikens and named in honor of Joseph Wright, a prominent Waterloo businessman. When they left for Elmira on April 30, the soldiers were seen off with a festive parade and formal public leave-taking. Becker's *History of Waterloo* described the situation as follows: "Banners and flags were floating from windows, trees, porticos and house-tops. Captain Aikens was presented with a beautiful sword and sash. Waterloo ladies sewed a 9 by 12 foot silk flag and many sets of shirts and stockings, etc. for the soldiers."[7] Clearly, it can be said that Seneca County "answered the call" at the outbreak of the Civil War in April 1861. By the end of 1861, nearly three hundred men had joined the ranks of the Union forces. Patriotic fervor for the defense of the Union was intense. The intensity of this fervor would be severely tested as the Civil War dragged on for four years.

Chapter 2
THE THIRTY-THIRD NEW YORK VOLUNTEERS

The Thirty-third New York Volunteers was one of the first regiments that answered President Lincoln's call for volunteers following the surrender of Fort Sumter in mid-April 1861. They were not professional soldiers but rather farmers and those involved in other occupations. Although they served only two years, there are many noteworthy accomplishments.

The Thirty-third Regiment was led by Colonel Robert F. Taylor of Rochester. The regiment suffered heavy losses in the Battles of Antietam, Fredericksburg and Chancellorsville and participated in many other smaller battles and skirmishes. Surviving members of the regiment returned home in early June 1863. Several of these returning soldiers reenlisted in other military units.[8]

The Wright Guards of Waterloo

One company of enlisted soldiers from Waterloo and two from Seneca Falls made up three of the ten companies that formally became the Thirty-third New York Volunteers, mustered into service on July 3, 1861, at Elmira. What became known as Company C of the Thirty-third Regiment began as eighty-six men who were sworn into service at Waterloo on April 26, 1861. They were first known as the Wright Guards, organized by Captain John

F. Aikens and named in honor of Joseph Wright, a prominent Waterloo businessman who provided the equipment for these enlistees. When they left for Elmira on April 30, the soldiers took with them a beautiful nine- by twelve-foot silk flag sewn by Waterloo ladies, who also gave the men eighty flannel and fifty cotton shirts, fifty pairs of woolen stockings and eighty bags containing buttons, needles, thread, bandages, lint and a Testament.[9]

TWO SENECA FALLS COMPANIES

The two companies consisting primarily of men from Seneca Falls were Companies A and K. Company A was organized by Edwin J. Tyler, a prominent Seneca Falls lawyer. Within the first week, eighty men had enlisted. They elected George M. Guion as their captain, with Edwin Tyler as first lieutenant. The Seneca Falls ladies sewed a flag that was presented to the company before it left for Elmira on May 13, 1861.

Patrick McGraw, who had served in the British armed forces for fifteen years prior to emigrating from Ireland to Seneca Falls in 1853, organized a second company of Seneca Falls residents. This company, Company K, consisted primarily of Irish immigrants from Seneca Falls.

George M. Guion was captain of one of the first companies of Seneca Falls men. *Seneca Falls Historical Society*.

Patrick McGraw organized a company of primarily Irish immigrants in Seneca Falls. *Seneca Falls Historical Society.*

A group of the Seneca Falls volunteers actually consisted of a band that officially became part of the band of the Thirty-third Volunteers when it was organized in Elmira.

Three Noteworthy Stories

Three especially noteworthy stories are associated with the Seneca County companies of the Thirty-third Regiment. The first story involves Private Richard Van Dusen of Company A. On July 20, 1861, he was guarding the Chain Bridge over the Potomac River. The Thirty-third Regiment had been deployed less than two weeks earlier to help protect the area surrounding our nation's capital. On July 20, President Lincoln and Pennsylvania governor Andrew Greg Curtin (great-great uncle of the late Harry Curtin, who was a resident of Lodi in Seneca County) and some others had traveled by carriage to visit Union troops across the Potomac River in Virginia. As they were returning to Washington via the Chain Bridge, Private Van Dusen stopped the carriage and demanded that he be shown the required "General McClellan's pass." Someone in the carriage said they didn't have such a pass because President Lincoln was in the carriage. Private Van Dusen wouldn't let the carriage proceed across the bridge without the required pass. So, the carriage group turned back to where they had been visiting troops, secured the required pass and returned to the bridge. Private Van Dusen then let the carriage group cross the bridge. Soon after that, one of McClellan's aides rode up to Private Van Dusen, and the faithful private was promoted to corporal on the spot.

Private Joseph Finnegan of Ovid died in an unfortunate incident within the camp of Company K on Christmas Eve 1861. Private Finnegan got into a dispute with Corporal John Tobin. Soon after this, Finnegan attempted to extinguish a fire in "a sort of ravine" by shoveling dirt into the fire. Tobin was sitting at the fireplace nearby, eating his supper, and inadvertently some of the dirt was thrown into Tobin's coffee. Tobin grabbed the shovel and struck Finnegan on the head. Finnegan bled profusely. The surgeon tried to dress the wound, but the hospital was full. Finnegan died in the captain's tent. Finnegan was a forty-one-year-old shoemaker who left behind a widow and six children.

On a happier note, Dr. Richard J. Curran of Seneca Falls was one of two soldiers in the Thirty-third Regiment to receive the Medal of Honor. He enlisted as a private in Company K and was the only medical officer present on the battlefield when the Battle of Antietam began on September 17, 1862. He set up a "field hospital" behind some stacks of straw just one hundred yards or so from the battle lines. Despite several requests to move back, he continued his medical work the rest of the day and night, saving many lives and improving the chances of many others.[10]

SOME LETTERS SENT HOME BY SENECA COUNTY SOLDIERS

On September 19, 1862, Captain G.M. Guion of Company A wrote a letter to the editor of the *Seneca Falls Reveille* in which he commented on the Battle of Sharpsburg, which had taken place two days earlier. He reported that Charles P. Siegfred and Frank Reynolds had been killed, that six others had been wounded and that one was still missing. The full brigade lost about 350 men, of which 44 were from the Thirty-third. He went on to say:

> *I cannot speak too highly of the firmness and unflinching bravery displayed by those under my command during the entire action, and especially while under the fire of the enemy's artillery and infantry. All did nobly, and none more so than those whose names are mentioned above, fully sustaining their well earned reputation of "veterans." The remains of the two who fell while gallantly fighting for the cause so dear to us all were removed from the field and buried in a neighboring cemetery. The wounded are all in the hospitals receiving the best possible attention.*[11]

However, not all of the letters that soldiers wrote to family back in Seneca County contained such dramatic accounts. Frequently the letters functioned much like a back-and-forth conversation. An example of this is the March 2, 1863 letter of William H. Green of Company C, in which he answered a question about his food raised by his father in a recent letter:

> *You asked me about my food and the quantities of rations; I would say that they are as good as one would ask for. "Old Joe" has ordered that we shall*

have four rations of fresh soft bread per week, two of fresh potatoes, and two of desiccated vegetables, or potatoes instead; as good coffee as any one can wish for and salt beef, and as good pork as any farmer in old Seneca can produce.

Sutlers of the Thirty-third Regiment

Mr. R.H. Dorsey of Seneca Falls and O.G. Judd of Geneva were appointed sutlers of the Thirty-third Regiment. They had the responsibility to "furnish the men with such supplies as they may need and the army regulations will permit."[12] When their term of service was up, many of the Seneca County men who served in the Thirty-third Regiment enlisted in other regiments.

Chapter 3

CAMP SWIFT: GENEVA'S CIVIL WAR MOBILIZATION CAMP

Starting in 1862, many Finger Lakes area soldiers who served in the Civil War were mustered into service at Camp Swift in Geneva, in neighboring Ontario County. The camp was located where a portion of the Tops Plaza currently exists—that area at the corner of Hamilton Street and White Springs Road. The camp was to be used to assemble local enlistees and provide them limited training and then ship them south to be soldiers in the war effort. Two major regiments of troops who departed

This plaque was never placed in the shopping center constructed on the former site of Camp Swift. *Geneva Historical Society.*

from Camp Swift were the 126th New York Volunteers and the 148th New York Volunteers.

History of Camp Swift

Camp Swift was founded in July 1862 after President Lincoln expressed the need for 300,000 more Union troops to fight what had clearly become a prolonged conflict with the secessionist Southern states. On July 11, 1862, a war committee appointed for New York's twenty-sixth senatorial district, consisting of Ontario, Seneca and Yates Counties, met in Geneva to make plans. According to the *Geneva Gazette* and the *Geneva Courier*, the committee selected the site—the former White Springs Trotting Park—as "just the place for drilling raw recruits." The racetrack site was chosen because it was located one mile from the center of the village, had an excellent water supply and was enclosed with a high fence.[13]

The selection of this site raised some serious opposition. The *Geneva Gazette* reported that an opposition group published a circular listing several reasons why the camp should not be located at the trotting park. One of the main reasons was the fear that recruits would be allowed to drink because the park's owner had a license to sell liquor. The *Gazette* noted that the liquor license applied to a house off the racecourse and that the soldiers would not have access to it unless they had permission from the commanding officer of the camp. The *Gazette* went on to argue that it would be better to have the soldiers at liberty drinking nearby the camp than to "have the soldiers passing through Main Street to reach the grog shops in the north part of the village." Stephen O'Malley, the curator of collections for the Geneva Historical Society in 1987, said that the main reason behind the objections to this site was that many people didn't want to lose their racetrack.[14]

Construction of the barracks and other camp buildings began in August 1862. The camp was named after Geneva's most renowned military resident at the time—General Joseph Gardner Swift. He was the first graduate of West Point Military Academy in 1802 and served as its superintendent from 1812 to 1817. He had also served as chief engineer of the U.S. Army. While fighting in the War of 1812, he earned the rank of brigadier general. Following his military service, he moved to Geneva and taught at Hobart College.

The district war committee had some difficulty in filling the position of commanding officer of the camp. Initially the post was offered to Senator Charles Folger of Geneva, who declined the offer. Next to decline was D.A. Ogden of Penn Yan. Eliakim Sherrill then agreed to take on the job. Sherrill was a former congressman from Ulster County who had acquired a farm in Geneva to live out his retirement.[15]

The 126th New York Volunteers

The 126th New York Volunteer Regiment was organized in the state's twenty-sixth senatorial district. Company A was the first company of the 126th to rendezvous at Camp Swift on August 4, 1862. In a note dated August 12, Deborah King of Romulus wrote to explicitly give her eighteen-year-old son, Clement King, permission to "volunteer in some good company in the defense of his country." In reaction to her note, Lieutenant John F. Brough wrote, "The above speaks volumes, would to God that all mothers of our land were prompted to lay upon the alter [*sic*] of their country, at least one of their sons."[16] The 126th was officially mustered into military service on August 22. On August 26–just four days after being mustered into service—the 126th Regiment "marched down through the streets of Geneva to the boat landing and embarked on the old *Elmira* (a steamship) for Watkins, the first stage of its journey to the front. Reaching Baltimore the following day, it was assigned for duty at Harpers Ferry..." Within three weeks of its departure from Camp Swift, many of the 126th Regiment were either killed or taken prisoner when Confederate forces attacked Harpers Ferry.[17]

The 148th New York Volunteers

Following the departure of the 126th Regiment from Camp Swift, the 148th New York Volunteers Regiment began training there. It was mustered into service on September 14. On September 22, the 148th marched down to the boat landing and departed on three steamboats for Watkins. One of the soldiers in Company A was John L. Hoster of Canoga.

Recent Festivities

The contribution of Camp Swift to the Union victory in the Civil War has not been completely forgotten. As part of the 1978 Geneva Festival, the "Town & Country Plaza," as it was then known, was renamed "Camp Swift." During the week of July 4–12, 1987, the city of Geneva celebrated the bicentennial of the U.S. Constitution in "Festival '87." The shopping plaza was once again temporarily "renamed" Camp Swift. Mayor Frank Cecere presented plaza owner Emil Muller with a facsimile of a plaque denoting the establishment of Camp Swift 125 years earlier. At the formal ceremonies, Michael Wajda, the executive director of the Geneva Historical Society, gave a brief description of the camp and its history. He added that it was not known when the camp stopped being utilized. The plaque is currently at the Geneva Historical Society.[18] No pictures of Camp Swift are known to exist today.

Chapter 4

THE 126TH NEW YORK VOLUNTEERS

MUSTERED INTO SERVICE AT CAMP SWIFT IN GENEVA

In early July 1862, President Lincoln issued a call for 300,000 men to join the Union forces. By spring 1862, there was serious concern about the progress of the war—particularly that it had not resulted in the expected quick Northern victory. In New York State, each state senatorial district had a quota of volunteers to recruit. There were state and federal bounties to encourage men to enlist.[19]

On July 15, 1862, Colonel Eliakim Sherrill was authorized to raise a regiment in the counties of Ontario, Seneca and Yates, which composed the New York State's twenty-sixth senatorial district. Companies A and B came from Yates County; C and I from Seneca County; D, H and K from Ontario Country; E from Geneva and Rushville; F from Ontario and Seneca Counties; and G from Ontario, Seneca and Yates Counties. Volunteers were mustered into service at Camp Swift in Geneva on August 22, 1862. On Tuesday, August 26, a total of 39 officers and 956 enlisted men left Camp Swift and marched through downtown Geneva to the docks. It is estimated that a crowd of 8,000 to 10,000 thousand came to see them off.[20] They traveled on steamboats *P.H. Field*, *S.T. Arnot* and *D.S. Magee* south on Seneca Lake to Watkins Glen. From there, they traveled by rail to Elmira. At the depot in Elmira, they received their tents, a .58-caliber Springfield rifle each and rations consisting of two loaves of bread, two slices of meat and two pieces of cheese. At sundown, they left on the Northern Central Railroad train and arrived at Harrisburg, Pennsylvania, at 6:30 a.m. on Wednesday, August 27. They then traveled to York and arrived at Baltimore at 1:30 p.m. At about 6:30 p.m., they boarded a train bound for Sandy Hook Station, Virginia, to relieve militia at Harpers Ferry. They arrived at Sandy Hook Station at midnight and spent the rest of the night cramped in their railroad cars. They arrived at Harpers Ferry at about 9:00 a.m. on Thursday, August 28.[21]

Surrender at Harpers Ferry—But Soon Back into Service

Given the geography of the area and the lack of sufficient Union defenses, the Union arsenal at Harpers Ferry was very vulnerable to Confederate attack. On September 15, 1861, the regiment surrendered. A force of eleven thousand soldiers, including the 126th, the 39th, the 111th and the 125th, was paroled with the garrison soldiers at Harpers Ferry and sent to Camp Douglas prison camp in Chicago, Illinois. After spending a few weeks there, the 126th Regiment and other regiments were then exchanged and rearmed. They became known as Casey's Division. They went into camp at Union Mills. On June 25, 1863, they were assigned as the 3rd Brigade of the 3rd Division of the 2nd Corps. They participated in all the battles in which the Army of the Potomac was engaged.[22]

Gettysburg

If the reputation of the 126th was tarnished because of what happened at Harpers Ferry, the regiment more than cleared its name by its distinguished actions at Gettysburg. The 3rd Brigade, of which the 126th was a part, reached Gettysburg at 8:00 a.m. on July 2, 1863, and was formed in line on the crest of the ridge south of Ziegler's Grove and the Bryan House.[23] Today in that area stands the monument to the 126th New York Infantry Regiment.

This monument to the 126th New York Volunteers was erected at the Gettysburg National Battlefield for their heroic fighting. *Walter Gable.*

The 126th New York was commanded in the Gettysburg fighting by Colonel Eliakim Sherrill. Sherrill took over the brigade on July 2, when Colonel Willard was killed near the Codori Farm. Lieutenant Colonel James M. Bull then took command of the regiment. Sherrill was mortally wounded at the location of the monument during Pickett's Charge on July 3.

Three soldiers of the 126th were awarded the Medal of Honor for their actions at Gettysburg. Captain Morris Brown Jr. of Company A and Private Jerry Wall of Company B both captured enemy battle flags. Sergeant George H. Dore of Company D was honored because when "the colors [were] struck down by a shell as the enemy were charging, this soldier rushed out and seized it, exposing himself to the fire of both sides."

In the fighting at Gettysburg, the 126th suffered the following casualties for officers: 30 killed, 5 wounded and 9 missing. For enlisted men, the numbers were 35 killed, 172 wounded and 10 missing. These figures are out of a total of 455 men who were engaged in battle.

One person characterized the 126th New York Volunteers as having been branded, along with its sister regiments in the brigade, as the "Harpers Ferry cowards" for their surrender—although through no fault of their own—with the garrison of Harpers Ferry during the Antietam campaign in 1862. Paroled but forced to spend a miserable winter in a Union prisoner of war camp in Chicago until exchanged, the brigade was looking for a chance to clear its name.[24]

THE FARMER BAND

One of the most celebrated musical organizations of the Union forces in the Civil War was composed largely of men from Farmer Village (present-day Interlaken) in the town of Covert in Seneca County. A few years before the start of the Civil War, Professor John M. Chadwick organized a band in Farmer Village. The following band members enlisted together in Company C of the 126th New York Volunteers on August 22, 1862: John M. Chadwick, George Chadwick, William R. Covert, Jonathan Grant, Eugene K. Holton, Richard Lockhart, F.M. Rappleye, Peter Rappleye, John L. Ryno, David Smith and Michael Stout. They became known as the 126th Regiment Band.

The band members were among the Union soldiers taken prisoner at Harpers Ferry in September 1862 and paroled to a camp in Chicago. After being exchanged, they were back as part of the Army of the Potomac at Union Mills, Virginia, on December 24, 1862. The band participated in several minor engagements. Band member David Smith, who was well known as a singer, died of small pox in camp at Centreville, Virginia, on January 6, 1863.

This band from Farmer Village (present-day Interlaken) became the regimental band for the 126th New York Volunteers. *Waterloo Historical Society*.

The members of the band were in Maryland when the first day of fighting at Gettysburg took place. Leaving their musical instruments behind, they were part of the Union forces that quickly marched to Gettysburg. Of the twelve members of the band that entered battle at Gettysburg, seven were wounded and one killed. Jonathan Grant, who had expressed a premonition that he was to be shot to death in the fighting, was killed on July 3, 1863, as he stood next to Michael Stout.[25] Eugene Holton was severely wounded in the hip at Gettysburg on July 3, 1863, and was discharged as a result.[26]

Starting on May 4, 1864, the 126th Regiment Band was reorganized as the main part of the 3rd Brigade Band and remained in that capacity for the rest of the war. The 3rd Brigade Band was the first band to play after the surrender of Confederate general Robert E. Lee at Appomattox Court House on April 9, 1865. One source described that day as follows:

> *The band had received orders, on the morning of that memorable day, to be ready at any moment to march to the front. About noon, the aide of General Miles rode up bearing the anticipated order, the musicians marched forward*

> *on the double quick, and took their positions between the skirmish lines. The Union batteries were anxiously awaiting the signal, and the moment the band began to play, the roar of cannon commenced. Gun after gun and battery after battery joined in the grand salute. The Union soldiers—tired from forced marches—almost forgot their weariness as they gave the last triumphal cheer, and the army of General Lee, brave but misguided, then knew that the old flag was to float in triumph over the South as well as the North, and that theirs was a lost cause.*[27]

On May 23 and 24, 1865, the 3rd Brigade Band was part of Grand Review of the victorious Union forces that paraded up Pennsylvania Avenue in Washington, D.C.[28] The band members were mustered out of military service on June 3, 1865, at Alexandria, Virginia.[29]

SENECA COUNTY MEN IN THE 126TH NEW YORK REGIMENT

Sergeant Tyler J. Snyder was among those killed at Gettysburg. He had enlisted in Captain John F. Aiken's Company G. He was shot in the right groin at Gettysburg on July 2 and died in the field hospital the next day. He is buried in the National Cemetery at Gettysburg. GAR Post 72 in Waterloo was named in his honor. Prior to his enlistment in 1862, he was a teacher.

Reverend Winfield Scott, who grew up in the Scotts Corners area in the town of Ovid, raised a company of his friends for service in Company C. Commissioned a captain of Company C, he was wounded at Harpers Ferry, captured, paroled and sent home. He returned to service and engaged in battle at Gettysburg. He was wounded at Spotsylvania in May 1864. There are reports that his wife, who was a noncommissioned army nurse, went to Washington, D.C., to meet personally with President Lincoln. Lincoln signed passes for her to enter Union lines and make arrangements to carry her husband back to their home in Farmer, where she nursed him back to health. Although he had to bear the handicaps from his war wounds the rest of his life, Scott became a missionary-preacher in the Far West. The communities of Winfield, Kansas, and Scottsdale, Arizona, are named in his honor.

Winfield Scott of Farmer (present-day Interlaken) in his Civil War uniform. Scott encouraged many young men in his Sunday school class to enlist in the 126th. *Waterloo Historical Society.*

Captain John Francis Aikens had served in the First New York Dragoons in the Mexican War. In 1860, he was an innkeeper in Waterloo. On July 29, 1861, he was discharged from the Wright Guards because of possible lung trouble. He reenlisted at Geneva on August 15, 1862, as the captain of Company G of the 126th New York Infantry. He and his company were taken prisoner at Harpers Ferry on September 15, 1862. He resigned as captain on March 4, 1863, and was discharged. Later in his life, he returned to the tavern business. He died on May 1, 1895, at the age of sixty-nine. He is buried in Maple Grove Cemetery in Waterloo.

Thomas Raynesford Lounsbury was born in Ovid, New York. He studied at the Ovid Academy and graduated Phi Beta Kappa from Yale University in 1859. He enlisted as a first lieutenant in Company C of the 126th on August 9, 1862, at Geneva, New York. At the Battle of Gettysburg, he was one of the few officers who suffered no injuries. He was discharged from military service in June 1865. He was an English professor at Yale University for thirty-six years.

Albert W. Porter enlisted as a private in Company C on July 28, 1862. He assisted in the recruiting of Seneca County men and became the second lieutenant of the company. He was discharged for disability on January 13, 1863, and operated a photograph gallery in Farmer (present-day Interlaken). Later, he was a manufacturer of leather goods in Lodi. He also was a musician. He died on October 16, 1897, in Lodi.[30]

Chapter 5

THE 148TH NEW YORK VOLUNTEERS

ORGANIZATION OF THE 148TH

Colonel William Johnson received authority on August 20, 1862, to recruit the 148th Regiment in what was then New York's twenty-sixth senatorial district. The regiment was organized in Geneva, with the recruits mustered into service for three years on September 14, 1862, at Camp Swift.

The 148th New York Volunteers enjoyed a rather peaceful first year and a half of active duty in the Suffolk, Virginia area. *Waterloo Historical Society.*

Company A recruits came from Seneca Falls, Fayette, Geneva and Canoga; Company B from Dundee, Starkey, Barrington and Milo; Company C from Phelps, Hopewell and Geneva; Company D from Geneva, Fayette and Varick; Company E from Ovid, Lodi, Romulus and Covert; Company F from Geneva, Rushville, Gorham, Rotter Center, Penn Yan and Middlesex; Company G from Geneva, Canandaigua and Naples; Company H from Waterloo, Seneca Falls and Tyre; Company I from Benton, Milo, Jerusalem, Torrey, Seneca, Branchport and Geneva; and Company K from Manchester, Bristol, East and West Bloomfield and Hopewell.[31]

THE JOURNEY INTO ACTIVE MILITARY SERVICE IN SOUTHERN VIRGINIA

On September 22, 1862, the soldiers of the 148th New York Volunteers left Camp Swift and marched down through the main business area of Geneva to the Seneca Lake docks. A large crowd bid them farewell. In a September 1862 letter, one soldier of the 148th said that he and his fellow soldiers

> *were intensely gratified to see that we had so many friends to speak the last consoling word, to utter the sad farewell, and to give the parting salute. We…shall never fail to remember their kindness, any more than our own emotions during the time that the boats lay at the wharf, and the moments which elapsed before the faces of the thousands of friends, congregated at the dock to view our safe exit from home, and to show their interest in the brave men who had displayed their willingness to meet death, if need be, to secure the nation's life, were lost to view.*[32]

At Watkins, the soldiers proceeded by train to Elmira, where they received their guns and camp and garrison equipage. From Elmira, the troops were transported by train, often in boxcars rather than passenger cars. In a letter to the editor of the *Seneca Falls Reveille*, one soldier of the 148th described his train trip south in September 1862 as follows:

> *After receiving our guns and two days rations, we started out late in the evening upon the Williamsport R.R. On Tuesday we passed Williamsport and the attractive capitol of Pennsylvania and arrived at about 5 P.M.*

at the thriving city of York. Here we received the kind hospitality of the people...and we were content to remain here until 10 P.M. when we moved on towards the great and prosperous city of Baltimore. We arrived at Baltimore at day-break, and marched through the city to the Washington Depot, where we remained until a soldier's breakfast could be provided by the Union Relief Association. Here we had an opportunity of seeing what kind of men we had to contend against, as there were about one hundred "Secesh" prisoners at the depot. Picture out in your imagination the appearance of one who had been removed to some filthy cavern for about the space of a year, deprived of all communication with beings of the human form, scantily supplied with food, and constantly haunted by demons, and you will have a very inadequate idea of the personale [sic] *of a rebel soldier. Clad in all sorts of uniforms, or, rather, in no uniform at all; some having no hats, others no coats, others no shoes nor stockings, wearing their hair and beard long and uncombed, covered with filth from head to foot, one would scarcely suppose they had ever beheld the first faint traces of civilization.*

Scarcely had we looked upon this woeful spectacle when one still more appalling was presented to our view. Three hundred [Union] *prisoners arrived from the capitol of the bogus Southern Confederacy, and it made one's blood boil to see the condition in which they had been left by the demons of the Secession. Deprived of every vestige of clothing, and supplied with barely food enough to sustain life, they looked as if they were just ready to fall into the grave. The story of their sufferings in Richmond was truly heart-rending. The good people of Baltimore furnished them with some articles of clothing, and they were sent upon the same train with ourselves to Washington. We arrived at the latter place at about 10 P.M. Wednesday* [September 24]. *Our quarters during the night were in the barracks near the depot.*[33]

This trip must have made a huge impression on many of the soldiers. Many of them had never been out of the Finger Lakes region, and most had undoubtedly never seen a prisoner of war before. Many were instilled with a hatred of the secessionist South, and seeing how those war prisoners were suffering did little to give them a more favorable view of the South.

From Washington, D.C., they journeyed to the greater Suffolk, Virginia area to begin their first military service. Until May 1864, they were engaged in noncombat duties in this Norfolk/Portsmouth area. The major Union base in that area was Fort Monroe. Much of their work involved guarding and processing the many Confederate prisoners of war and working on procuring and shipping supplies to units engaged in battle inland.

Active Fighting Starting in May 1864

Starting May 4, 1864, the 148th became involved in actual battle as part of General Butler's operations on the south side of the James River and against Petersburg and Richmond. The soldiers of the 148th were heavily engaged in battle at Cold Harbor. Several soldiers were taken prisoners in mid-June in the area near Gaines Mills. The 148th was involved in final assault on Petersburg in April 1865 and was at Appomattox Court House when Confederate general Robert E. Lee surrendered to Union general Ulysses S. Grant.

End of Active Service

The remaining soldiers of the 148th—which had become part of the 3rd Brigade, 1st Division, 24th Corps in March 1865, under the command of Colonel John B. Murray—were honorably discharged and mustered out of service on June 22, 1865, at Richmond, Virginia.

During its service, the 148th lost 2 officers and 63 enlisted men killed in action, 2 officers and 42 enlisted men due to wounds received in action and 2 officers and 156 enlisted men due to disease and other causes. These losses total 6 officers and 267 enlisted men. A total of 24 of the enlisted men died in the hands of the enemy.[34]

A total of five members of the 148th Regiment received the Medal of Honor: Private George A. Buchanan of Company G, who on September 29, 1864, took position in advance of the skirmish line and drove the enemy's cannoneers from their guns at the Battle of Chaffin's Farm near Richmond, Virginia, where he was mortally wounded; Private Richard C. Mangam of Company H, who captured the flag of the 8th Mississippi Infantry (CSA) at the Battle of Hatcher's Run in Virginia on April 2, 1865; Corporal Eugene M. Tinkham of Company H, who, though himself wounded, voluntarily left the rifle pits, crept out between the lines and exposed himself to the severe fire of the enemy's guns at close range in order to retrieve wounded and helpless comrades during action at Cold Harbor, Virginia, on June 3, 1864; (4) Corporal Edwin Van Winkle of Company C, who took position in advance of the skirmish line and drove the enemy's cannoneers from their guns at the Battle of Chaffin's Farm near Richmond, Virginia, on September 29, 1864; and Private Henry S. Wells of Company C, who, along with two comrades, took position in advance of the skirmish line and drove enemy gunners from their guns in action at the Battle of Chaffin's Farm.[35]

Colonel John B. Murray was instrumental in the establishment of a Memorial Day in Waterloo, New York, in 1866.

Chapter 6

OTHER REGIMENTS IN WHICH SENECA COUNTY MEN SERVED

In addition to the 33rd, 126th and 148th Regiments, Seneca County men served in several other regiments. These include the 19th New York Volunteer Infantry, the 15th New York Engineers, the 44th New York Volunteers, the 50th New York Engineers and the 75th New York Volunteers. Their stories are briefly told in this chapter.

THE NINETEENTH NEW YORK VOLUNTEER INFANTRY

The Nineteenth New York Volunteer Infantry was organized in Auburn, New York, and consisted primarily of Cayuga County residents, with some members from Seneca County. It called itself the "Seward Infantry" in honor of Lieutenant Colonel Clarence Seward of Auburn. Meanwhile, Captain John H. Ammon had been raising another fine company at Auburn, with twenty of the men being Seneca Falls residents. They reached Elmira on May 9 and were quartered in Beecher's church.[36]

On May 22, 1861, the various companies assembled in Elmira were organized as the Nineteenth New York Volunteer Infantry. The regimental officers elected were John S. Clark, colonel; Clarence A. Seward, lieutenant colonel; and James H. Ledlie, major.[37] Captain Ashcroft's company of Seneca Falls men became Company C of this Nineteenth New York Volunteers

Regiment. Although the men had enlisted for two years, an unauthorized Captain W.L. Elliott mustered the men of the Nineteenth into service for the United States for only three months.[38]

On June 5, 1861, the Nineteenth New York Volunteer Infantry left Elmira to help with the defense of Washington, D.C. On December 11, 1861, the designation of the regiment was changed to the Third Regiment New York Light Artillery.[39] Battery C (the renamed Company C) saw heavy guard and picket duty along the Potomac River but did not actively engage in any battle.[40] In spring 1862, the Third New York Artillery began service in North Carolina. Ashcroft and those soldiers who had enlisted for two years were mustered out of service at Elmira, New York, on June 2, 1863. A new Battery C, including the men of Company C who had enlisted for three years, was mustered into service on August 31, 1863. This newly organized Battery C joined the Third Artillery Regiment in New Berne, North Carolina, where it was equipped as heavy artillery, engaged in construction work at Fort Totten and participated in several expeditions into the surrounding country. It was active in fighting in March and April 1865, engaging the enemy at several different points, notably Southwest Creek, Wise's Forks and Bennett House. Battery C was mustered out of service at Syracuse, New York, on July 14, 1865. During its service, the total loss of the entire regiment was 189 members killed, wounded or missing.[41]

THE FIFTEENTH NEW YORK ENGINEERS

The Fifteenth New York Engineers was accepted by the State of New York on May 9, 1861, and organized in New York City as the Fifteenth New York Infantry. The regiment, commanded by Colonel J. McLeod Murphy, left New York on June 29, 1861, to begin service as infantry in the Washington, D.C. area. Intended to be an engineer regiment, it was converted to that arm of the service by the War Department on October 25, 1861. It then functioned as an engineer brigade in the Army of the Potomac. In March 1862, it was moved to the Virginia Peninsula, where it would be present for Lee's surrender to Grant at Appomattox Court House on April 9, 1865.[42] It was also involved in the Battle of Gettysburg on July 1–3, 1863. A large stone monument has been erected on Cemetery Ridge in honor of the Fifteenth New York Engineers. Losses suffered by this regiment total 3 officers and

Monument for the Fiftieth Engineers and Fifteenth New York Volunteers at Gettysburg National Battlefield. *Walter Gable.*

126 enlisted men, with 1 enlisted man dying in the hands of the enemy.[43] Of these losses, 4 enlisted men were killed in action, 1 enlisted man died of wounds received in action and 121 enlisted men and 3 officers died of disease and other causes.

Companies G and I[44] included sixty men from Seneca County. These men had volunteered for service in the Fiftieth New York Engineers in response to President Lincoln's call in 1864 for a massive number of volunteers to finish the war. However, so many volunteered for service in the Fiftieth New York Engineers that these sixty Seneca Falls area residents were assigned instead to the Fifteenth New York Engineers.[45] Most of these men were veterans of other units who had volunteered again, motivated probably as much by the large enlistment bonuses as by their patriotic feelings.

These Seneca County men were mustered into service in Camp Seward at Auburn and reached Elmira on October 3, 1864. On October 8, they left Elmira for City Point, which was the headquarters of the Union army in the siege of Petersburg. They spent the winter laying out and building fortifications and erecting hospitals for the Second and Ninth Army Corps. From time to time, they were brought to the front to line new works. On April 2, 1865, they were actively engaged in extinguishing fires in Petersburg. As Union troops advanced westward from there, they were constructing bridges for the passage of troops and trains. On May 1, they were ordered to Washington. On their march, they passed through Richmond, forming a part of the forces that would take part in the grand review of troops marching through the Rebel stronghold on May 6.[46]

Companies G and I were among those mustered out of service at Washington, D.C., on June 13, 1865.[47]

THE FORTY-FOURTH NEW YORK VOLUNTEER INFANTRY

The first Union officer to die in the Civil War was Colonel Elmer Ellsworth. Ellsworth had been a member of the New York Fire Zouave Regiment. To honor him, it was decided to raise a regiment consisting of one man from each town and ward in the state of New York chosen by the residents of that town or ward. According to the circular sent to each town, each candidate was to be "an able-bodied man, unmarried, temperate, at least five feet eight inches in height, of good moral character, and bring credentials that he represented some town or ward in the State, and pay in to the regimental fund the sum of $20." The regiment was designated as the Forty-fourth New York Volunteers but was popularly known as the "People's Ellsworth Regiment."

The regiment was mustered into service on September 24, 1861, for three years. On October 24, the regiment's some 1,061 men, dressed neatly in Zouave uniforms, left their barracks in Albany for New York City. Arriving there, they marched down Broadway in column, receiving an inspiring and hearty reception from the people of the city. They then proceeded by railroad cars to Washington, D.C., where they spent their first night on doorsteps and sidewalks. The following morning, they marched down Pennsylvania Avenue, where President Lincoln reviewed the regiment as it passed by the White House. They were assigned to Butterfield's Brigade of Porter's Division. They spent the fall and winter in squad, company, battalion and brigade drills and eased into the routine of camp life.

The regiment was involved in the actions of the Army of the Potomac. Upon the evacuation of Yorktown on May 5, 1862, the regiment was detached from the brigade to garrison Yorktown. The regiment petitioned to be reassigned back to the battlefront, and the soldiers soon got their wish. In the Battle of Malvern Hill on July 1, 1862, the regiment suffered 99 killed and wounded out of the 225 men engaged in battle. General Butterfield had ordered them to charge the enemy. Lieutenant Colonel Rice, who was in command of the regiment, said to his men, "Forty-fourth, I want you to charge today as you never charged before." His wish was fully gratified. As his men continued to advance, Rice yelled out, "Men, we are Christians and we can die." The enemy were driven from their advanced position and pursued as they retreated in confusion and disorder.

In the Battle of Second Bull Run, the regiment lost in killed and wounded 71 of the 160 officers and men engaged. On about October 1, 1862, the numbers of the regiment were augmented by the addition of two new companies. One consisted almost entirely of students of the Albany Normal School and was commanded by Captain Kimball, one of their professors.

On the night of June 30, 1863, the regiment with the balance of Barnes's Division was encamped at Union, Maryland. At an early hour on July 1, they resumed their march to Hanover, Pennsylvania, arriving there at sundown. Hearing the news of the first day of fighting at Gettysburg on July 1, 1863, the Forty-fourth regiment and the balance of Barnes's Division proceeded as quickly as they could to Gettysburg. That afternoon, they arrived at Little Round Top just a few minutes before the attack from the Confederate forces. Colonel Rice, who had assumed command of the brigade, said in his battle report, "Massing two or three brigades of his (Confederate) force, he tried for an hour in vain to break the lines of the Forty-fourth New York and Eighty-third Pennsylvania, charging again and again within a few yards of those unflinching troops." The next day, the men of the Forty-fourth were relieved and took position in reserve for the third day of fighting at Gettysburg. The Forty-fourth lost in killed and wounded more than 34 percent of the men engaged in battle. General Longstreet, in his book *From Manassas to Appomattox*, wrote, "We were on Little Round Top grappling for the crowning point. The brigade commanders there, Vincent and Weed, were killed, also Battery Commander Hazlett and others, but their troops were holding to their work as firmly as the mighty boulders that helped them." Lieutenant Colonel Conner, who had assumed command of the Forty-fourth, wrote in his battle report, "It affords me great pleasure to be able to state that both officers and men behaved with greatest coolness and bravery, not a single case of cowardice having come to my attention."

Those in the regiment who had completed their three years of service—approximately 100 out of the original 1,061—were mustered out at Albany on September 24, 1864. Those who were still in service were consolidated with the 144th New York and 146th New York. The 44th New York was officially mustered out of service on October 11, 1864.[48]

James Hitchcock of Seneca Falls was a member of the Forty-fourth New York Regiment. An 1862 letter to the editor of the *Seneca County Courier* telling of the fighting near Richmond, Virginia, at the Battle of Hanover Court House on May 27, 1862, had this to say about the heroism of James Hitchcock:

> *I must allude to the splendid and noble behavior of James Hitchcock of Seneca Falls. He displayed as much courage, noble daring and heroism as any man possibly could throughout the fight, until he was severely wounded. The old bullet-riddled flag, which had been so gallantly defended by our brave and noble boys, fell to the ground. The Ensign was instantly killed. Two others who had volunteered to carry the old emblem had fallen; Hitchcock rushed forward as we were exposed to a most galling and murderous fire and raised the flag, asking Col. Rice, if he would permit him to take charge of that old banner? With his consent, he rushed forward in advance of his Regiment, and while waving it in the face of the enemy, was struck by a musket ball in the leg inflicting a severe wound, though not so serious as to make amputation necessary. Holding on to the flag-staff and waving the flag as he went limping along on his wounded limb toward Col. Rice, refusing to deliver it to any one save the Colonel himself. He resigned it into his hands, amidst the praises of every officer and man in the Regiment. He was complimented by the Colonel commanding, and promoted on the spot to Sergeant in his Company. Col. Rice alluded to his conduct as a model for every soldier.*[49]

Edward Payson Chapin was born in Waterloo, New York, on August 16, 1831. He was working as an attorney in Buffalo when the Civil War began. In late August 1861, he joined Company A of the 44th New York Volunteer Infantry. By January 2, 1862, he had been promoted to major. He was seriously wounded in action in May 1862 at Hanover Court House in Virginia. He returned to Buffalo to recover and was promoted to lieutenant colonel, at which time he was instrumental in raising a new regiment—the 116th

New York Volunteers—of Erie County men. At the Battle of Port Hudson (in Louisiana) on May 27, 1863, Chapin was hit in the knee early in the battle. Then, as he approached the Confederate line, he was struck in the head by a minié ball and was killed. His military service record reports that "he was killed in action while gallantly leading his men in the assault of Port Hudson." He died one year to the day from his Virginia wounding. His father, Ephraim Chapin, who was the pastor of the Waterloo Presbyterian Church, was sent Edward's posthumous promotion to brigadier general by President Lincoln (effective May 27, 1863, the day of his death). Edward Chapin was buried in Waterloo's Maple Grove Cemetery. Chapin Parkway in Buffalo was named in his memory.[50]

John B. Murray in his military uniform before he became a brigadier general. At the time of the initial Memorial Day events in Waterloo, Murray was the Seneca County clerk. *Waterloo Historical Society.*

Fiftieth New York Engineers

On July 26, 1861, Colonel Charles B. Stuart received authority to recruit a regiment of engineers, which he proceeded to organize at Elmira. On September 20, 1861, the companies he organized were designated the Fiftieth New York. It was a regiment of engineers, pontoniers, sappers and miners and became known as "Stuart's Independent Volunteers." One of the recruiting places for Company B was Waterloo, while Ovid and Seneca Falls were recruiting grounds for Company K.[51] At the outbreak of the Civil War, the Union army had only one battalion of engineers. Stuart, who was promoted to the rank of general, was an eminent engineer, so it is not surprising that his engineering regiment consisted of men qualified to build railroads, run locomotives and conduct trains. The men who enlisted in this regiment ranged from common laborers to lawyers, as well as experienced engineers.[52]

The Fiftieth New York was on duty at Alexandria, Virginia, and Washington, D.C., until March 18, 1862, as part of Woodbury's Brigade, Army of the Potomac. In early April 1862, it became part of the Army of the Potomac's Engineer Brigade in the Virginia Peninsula and was soon engaged in the siege of Yorktown. The regiment took part in the famous Battles of Gettysburg and Cold Harbor, the fall of Petersburg and the Appomattox Court House campaign before being mustered out at Washington, D.C., on June 13–14, 1865.[53] The regiment lost 17 to wounds and 214 to disease and other causes.[54]

One of the Seneca County men who served in Company K of the 50th Regiment was Captain John B. Murray of Waterloo. On July 22, 1862, he resigned from the 50th Regiment to assist in organizing the 148th Regiment, which was then being organized in Seneca County and neighboring counties of Ontario and Yates.

Another Seneca County soldier in Company K was Lieutenant James H. McDonald, who was promoted to the rank of captain with the departure of Murray. On August 13, 1862, McDonald's Company K was ordered to the Chickahominy River, some twenty miles distant, to prepare the way for the army to evacuate the peninsula. Arriving at Charles City Court-House, they found a gallows standing in the courthouse yard. An aged Negro told them that it had been used to hang several of his race who had attempted to escape slavery. Company K men used their axes to destroy the gallows and used the wood as a campfire to heat their coffee. Each of the soldiers was obliged to carry weapons and forty rounds, an axe or spade, three days' rations and a knapsack. Many soldiers found this load too heavy for the rapid marching and heavy roadwork they were doing. They approached a young man on his walk to mill with a mule team. The soldiers took the wagon and filled it with their knapsacks. Lightened of their loads, the men pushed forward more rapidly, repairing several bridges on their route, and reached the mouth of Chickahominy River at Barnett's Ferry the next day. There, they assisted Captain Spaulding in laying a pontoon bridge nearly 1,600 feet in length. When General McClellan arrived on August 17, he declared the bridge to be the longest known to him. For three days and nights, this bridge was occupied by the passing of infantry, cavalry, artillery and interminable supply lines.[55]

In early 1863, the *Seneca County Courier* reported on a special presentation that was made to Captain James H. McDonald:

> *Capt. Jas. H. McDonald, of the 50th Regiment, received on Monday evening, a very substantial present at the hands of his fellow-citizens, for gallant and meritorious conduct as a soldier. The presentation took place at Union Hall*

> [in Seneca Falls] *and was witnessed by a large number in attendance. The meeting was organized by selecting A.J. Goffe, Esq., as chairman, after which Hon. Benson Owen, in a speech suitable to the occasion, presented the Captain with a pair of Colt's Revolvers, of the best and most improved patern* [sic]. *A purse of $50 was also presented. Capt. McDonald replied in a brief, modest and appropriate speech, thanking his fellow-citizens for their flattering testimonials presented. It will be remembered that Capt. McDonald was seriously wounded while throwing a pontoon bridge across the Rappahannock the day previous to the battle of Fredericksburg, his left arm being pierced by a musket ball. He has not entirely recovered from the effects of the wound. He left, however, for his Regiment on the noon train Wednesday.*[56]

The Seventy-fifth New York Volunteers

The Seventy-fifth New York Volunteers were recruited in Seneca and Cayuga Counties in early September 1861 by Colonel John A. Dodge at Camp Cayuga in Auburn. The regiment was officially organized with nine companies on November 26, 1861.[57] Companies K and I were partly composed of men from Seneca Falls and Waterloo. On December 6, the men left for duty at Fort Pickens, Florida. Arriving at Santa Rosa on December 13, they proceeded to lay out a new camp, which they named Seward.[58] The Seventy-fifth was involved in the occupations of Pensacola, Florida, and New Orleans, Louisiana; the siege of Port Hudson (May 27–June 14, 1863), during which it suffered 107 casualties; and the siege of Sabine Pass (September 8, 1863), during which it suffered 85 casualties. On June 28, 1864, the men of the Seventy-fifth were assigned to the First Brigade, Second Division of the Nineteenth Army Corps and relocated to the Shenandoah Valley in Virginia. In early 1865, they were assigned to the First Brigade, First Division, Tenth Army Corps with provost duty in Savannah, Georgia. They were mustered out of service on August 23, 1865.[59]

One of several Seneca County soldiers who served in the Seventy-fifth New York Volunteers was Lieutenant William E. Avery of Farmer. The *Farmerville Sentinel* in June 1863 printed the following letter from Captain Fitch at Brashear City, Louisiana, to Honorable E.B. Morgan, telling of the death of Lieutenant William E. Avery:

It is with a sad heart that I write you that WILLIAM E. AVERY is no more. He was instantly killed by a bullet passing through his heart while gallantly leading his company on the works at Port Hudson. I have caused his remains to be enclosed in a metallic case, and put in the receiving vault in New Orleans, subject to my order. In consequence of his lying on the battle field two days before he could be removed, his remains could not be embalmed. His trunk and sword are here at my house. I telegraphed the Purser of the Morning Star at the Passes, to let you know immediately on her arrival in New York. I would suggest some one coming here for the remains, in about six weeks, and if possible an escort will be sent with him. Our regiment is reported badly cut up. I do not know the particulars, as all news from the field of battle is suppressed. We have lost a large number of officers of all grades. Please say to Mr. Avery, all that could be done for Will, was done, and I assure you if he had been my brother, I could feel the loss no greater than I do.

Please inform me as to the wishes of his father, and they shall be faithfully executed.

I am, Sir, Yours respectfully,
HENRY B. FITCH, Capt., 75th N.Y.

That same newspaper went on to report that this information "spread like an electric shock through the village and surrounding country where Lieut. Avery had been so long and favorably known. He was one of the first of our young men who enlisted to resist the inroads of treason and rebellion." The sword that was alluded to in the letter was a gift of the ladies of Farmer at the time of Lieutenant Avery's departure for military service. Lieutenant Avery had been in command of the company at times and "was held in high esteem both among officers and his own men, and from various sources we hear him commended as a genial friend and daring soldier." He had recruited many of the men who served with him.[60]

Chapter 7

MEDAL OF HONOR RECIPIENTS FROM SENECA COUNTY

WHAT IS THE MEDAL OF HONOR?

The Medal of Honor is the United States of America's highest military honor, awarded for personal acts of valor above and beyond the call of duty. The medal is awarded by the president of the United States in the name of Congress to U.S. military personnel only. There are three versions of the medal: one for the U.S. Army, one for the U.S. Navy and one for the U.S. Air Force. Personnel of the U.S. Marine Corps and Coast Guard receive the navy version.

On December 9, 1861, Iowa senator James W. Grimes introduced S. No. 82, a bill to "promote the efficiency of the Navy" by authorizing the production and distribution of "medals of honor" for navy personnel in the Civil War. The bill was passed on December 21 and authorized two hundred such medals to be produced. It is probably because General Winfield Scott, commander of the U.S. Army, personally opposed any such medal—thinking they were too much like what European countries did—that a similar program was not enacted for the U.S. Army until July 12, 1862.

It was on May 24, 1861, that Private Francis Edwin Brownell performed the first action—in Alexandria, VA—to merit the Medal of Honor.

The first medals ever to be presented occurred on March 25, 1863. Secretary of War Edwin Stanton presented medals to six of the surviving members of Andrews' Raiders.

On February 5, 1917, the Medal of Honor review board struck the names of 911 medal recipients from the honor roll. The stricken names included all the 864 medals awarded to the Twenty-seventh Maine, 29 members of President Lincoln's funeral guard and 6 civilians (ineligible because of their civilian status), including Dr. Mary Walker, who is the only female to be awarded the medal. (Her medal was restored on June 10, 1977.)[61]

In 1990, Congress designated March 25 as National Medal of Honor Day.[62]

As of March 1, 2014, a total of 3,480 Medals of Honor have been awarded for 3,475 different acts of heroism performed by 3,461 different individuals. A total of 1,522 were awarded for actions in the Civil War.[63] Roughly a quarter of them were awarded to Irish immigrants.[64]

Dr. Richard J. Curran of Seneca Falls

At least three Civil War soldiers from Seneca County received the Medal of Honor. One of these was Dr. Richard J. Curran of Seneca Falls. Curran was born on January 13, 1838, in Carrahill, County Clare, on the southwest coast of Ireland. In 1850, his parents, Richard and Catharine O'Mealy, brought him to America and settled in Seneca Falls. Upon graduating from Mynderse Academy, Richard worked in the drugstore of J.E. Clark. He began studying medicine in the office of Drs. Srually and Davis. He then went to Harvard Medical School, graduating in 1859. He did post-graduate work with Dr. Oliver Wendell Holmes, the great physician and author. In 1860, Dr. Curran returned to Seneca Falls.[65]

Shortly after the fall of Fort Sumter, Dr. Curran assisted in the formation of Companies A and K of the Thirty-third New York Infantry, consisting mainly of Seneca Falls men. On May 22, 1861, he enlisted as a private in Company K. In October 1861, he was promoted to hospital steward for the regiment. On August 15, 1862, he was promoted to assistant surgeon in the Third Brigade.[66] This was approximately one month before the famous Battle of Antietam on September 17, in which the Union army suffered over 12,000 casualties, including over 2,100 dead.

When the Third Brigade arrived at Antietam, it was quickly engaged in the fighting. Curran wrote, "I was the only medical officer present with the regiment at that time and in absence of orders [proceeded to set up a] field hospital" just one hundred yards or so from the battle lines. He spent the rest of the day and night saving many lives and improving the chances of many others. He later wrote, "During the severest of the fighting and later on I was told many times by the officers and men if I did not seek a place of safety I would surely be killed…When advised to go to the rear and to a place of safety, I could possibly have done so and all would have credited me with doing my duty, but I believed a great opportunity was at hand to render a marked service at a critical junction even though my life might well be the forfeit. I took the chance and humbly believe the service was rendered."[67]

Lieutenant Bernard Byrne of Company K wrote, "He [Curran] had the wounded taken to some stacks of straw near our lines, where they were afforded comparative protection, and here although under constant fire he worked unremittingly till night closed the battle. Dr. Curran on this occasion was worthy of all praise. Very many were saved by his skill and unaided attention."[68]

When the Thirty-third was mustered out in June 1863, Dr. Curran reenlisted as the assistant surgeon of the Sixth New York Cavalry, where he served until September 18, 1864. He then served as surgeon of the Ninth New York Cavalry until July 17, 1865, having been an eyewitness to Lee's surrender at Appomattox.

When he returned to Seneca Falls, he married Mary A. Rogers. Soon after getting married, the couple moved to Rochester and opened the drugstore of Curran and Goler on the corner of Main Street West and North Fitzhugh Street. According to the *Rochester Herald*, it soon became known as one of the best-equipped pharmacies in western New York. Following Mary's death in 1875, Curran became involved in Rochester's civil affairs. He was Rochester school commissioner for one year and then park commissioner for two years. He married Katie W. Whalen in 1881. He served in the state legislature in 1891 and then one term as mayor of Rochester.

In 1898, following years of prodding by many of his army comrades, Dr. Curran applied for the Medal of Honor. On March 22, 1898, he was awarded the Medal of Honor for "most distinguished gallantry in action." The letter of notification read:

> *At Antietam, Md., September 17, 1862, this officer, then Assistant Surgeon, 33^{d} New York Volunteers, and in charge of the Field Hospital*

> *of the 3d Brigade, 2d Division, 6th Army Corps, when urged by some of his comrades to remain in a place of safety in the rear as was his privilege, disregarded these requests and voluntarily exposed himself to very great danger by going to the fighting line, there succoring the wounded and helpless and conducting them to the Field Hospital. He remainded* [sic] *with the wounded throughout the battle at the Hospital, which was also within the range of the enemy's fire. The Brigade Commander, in his official report of the battle, particularly commends Assistant Surgeon Curran for his services and example.*

Curran died of heart failure on June 1, 1915. He was buried in Holy Sepulchre Cemetery in Rochester. George Contant, in his book *Path of Blood*, said that Dr. Richard J. Curran "remains a jewel in western New York's crown of great men."[69]

CORPORAL EUGENE TINKHAM OF WATERLOO

Few people can identify Eugene Tinkham as the Waterloo resident who earned the Medal of Honor for his Civil War exploits. He was a corporal in Company H of the 148th New York Infantry. He was cited for extraordinary heroism for his actions on June 3, 1864, in the battle at Cold Harbor, Virginia. The citation read, "Though himself wounded, Corporal Tinkham voluntarily left the rifle pits, crept out between the lines and, exposed to the severe fire of the enemy's guns at close range, brought within the lines two wounded and helpless comrades."

Cold Harbor was a twelve-day battle in which General Grant was launching a major assault against Lee's forces that were entrenched in the Richmond, Virginia area. Approximately 170,000 troops were involved on the two sides. There were 13,000 Union casualties and 5,000 Confederate casualties.

Eugene Tinkham was born in Sprague, Connecticut, in 1832 and died there in 1909. He is buried there in the New Hanover Cemetery. His gravestone wording uses his final rank of sergeant.

Tinkham was working as a spinner at the Seneca Knitting Mill in Seneca Falls in 1862. He enlisted in Waterloo when the 148th New York Regiment was mustered in in September 1862. The 148th Regiment was organized in Geneva, New York, on September 14, 1862, and was sent to Norfolk, Virginia, for garrison and guard duty. The 148th was involved in fighting in the Petersburg, Virginia area for almost a year.[70]

Hartwell Thomas Benton Compson of Seneca Falls

Hartwell Thomas Benton Compson was born on May 5, 1842, in Seneca Falls, New York, the second of thirteen children born to Jonas and Ruth Compson. On August 28, 1861, he enlisted at the age of eighteen as a private in Captain Sisson's company of the Eighth New York Cavalry.[71] He rose rapidly through the ranks and became regimental commander.

On March 2, 1865, he led his troops into battle at Waynesboro, Virginia. During fierce hand-to-hand combat, Major Compson and Captain Christopher Bruton personally captured the headquarters flag of Confederate general Jubal Early.[72] In that sharp battle, the Union forces took 1,500 prisoners, five pieces of artillery and ten Rebel flags.[73] Also captured was General Early's headquarters wagon, which contained all his official papers and records. An account of Compson's heroic actions in this battle is as follows:

> *It was a battle where the Eighth New York Cavalry, under the gallant leadership of Major Hartwell B. Compson, earned undying fame. The major himself performed wonderful feats of bravery and set an example which electrified his men and inspired them to deeds of splendid heroism. At the head of his troops who were selected to make the attack, he charged down the highway into Waynesboro. The enemy had five pieces of artillery in the roadway and had thrown up earthworks on each side of the road; behind these breastworks infantry was posted. He was at the head of his command with a color-bearer on one side and bugler on the other, when they struck the Confederate forces and a hand-to-hand fight took place. Just then General Early and his staff moved down their front to direct the movement of the Confederate forces. Coming upon Early's headquarters battle-flag he ordered the bearer to surrender. A fierce fight at close quarters ensued and finally a heavy blow with the sabre knocked his opponent from his horse and the flag was captured.*

Eugene Tinkham received the Medal of Honor for his actions during the battle at Cold Harbor, Virginia. *Library of Congress.*

> *Breaking through the Confederates, he moved his forces down toward South River and kept up the charge until he reached the bank. Seeing that the enemy were closing in on his rear and that his support did not come up, he crossed the river and found earthworks thrown up on the opposite side from which the enemy could have prevented their crossing had they occupied them. He at once dismounted his men and placed them in the Confederate earthworks. Then when* [General George] Custer [who was leading another company of Union soldiers] *pressed down upon the rebels they were forced to cross the river, where they were ordered to surrender. The result was that when the battle was over Colonel Compson's command alone had taken 800 prisoners, five pieces of artillery, 1,500 stands of small arms and eight battle-flags.*
>
> *Being needed no longer at the ford, Compson, who had noticed the enemy moving their wagon-trains over the mountains by way of Rock Fish Gap, followed with regiment, overhauled it and captured everything in sight.*[74]

A total of fourteen soldiers were awarded Medals of Honor as a result of this battle.[75] Unlike many of the men whose bravery was not recognized for decades, Compson received his medal within a month of the battle—on March 26, 1865.[76] His Medal of Honor citation included the following wording: "Capture of flag belonging to Gen. Early's headquarters."[77] The flag was a Confederate Second National flag measuring four feet by six feet and was presented by Compson to the secretary of war. The Federal government returned the flag to Virginia in 1906. It is in the possession of the Museum of the Confederacy in Richmond.[78]

After mustering out in June 1865, Compson worked as a U.S. marshal and postmaster. In 1885, he visited back in Seneca Falls and then was in the regular army stationed in Utah. In 1887, he was living in California and was appointed brigadier general of the Oregon National Guard.[79] He died on August 31, 1905, in Portland, Oregon, where he is buried in the Grand Army of the Republic Cemetery.[80]

Chapter 8

SOME SENECA COUNTY MEN WHO SERVED

At least 1,328 Seneca County men served in the Civil War. Because of space limitations, this chapter tells about only a few of these soldiers. These accounts provide some insights into the typical and not-so-typical experiences of many Civil War soldiers.

William Cross of Seneca Falls and His Five Sons in the Civil War

Many families had to make sacrifices as their men went off to war. For the Cross family of Seneca Falls, it was an especially noteworthy sacrifice in that William Henry Cross and his five eldest sons served in the Union army. Two died while in service. Three were wounded.

William Henry Cross was born in Green County, New York, on October 28, 1809. He married Lucy A. Boardman on December 23, 1833. She was born in Seneca Falls on April 21, 1818, the daughter of Deming Boardman. The 1840 U.S. census lists William H. Cross living in the town of Tyre. The U.S. censuses of both 1850 and 1860 show William Henry Cross as a farmer living in the town of Seneca Falls with his wife and children—six sons and three daughters.

On May 22, 1861—about six weeks after the fall of Fort Sumter—son Amos N. enlisted as a member of Company K of the Thirty-third New York Infantry. Amos was born on February 14, 1837, so he was twenty-four at the time of his enlistment. Like many Civil War soldiers, Amos had several illnesses. He was treated for diarrhea in the Regimental Hospital on November 28, 1861, and again on December 10, 1861. On January 12, 1862, he was treated for catarrh because of his bad cough. On September 11, 1862, he died in the General Hospital at Mill Creek near Fort Monroe, Virginia, with "debility" (the state of being weak or feeble). He was buried in the Hampton National Cemetery in Hampton, Virginia. There is also a gravestone with his name in Restvale Cemetery in Seneca Falls.

William Henry Cross himself enlisted at the age of fifty-three on September 16, 1861, in Company K of the Fiftieth New York Engineers as a carpenter. While on a scouting party, he suffered a broken tibia and fibula on his right leg in the process of jumping a ditch. He was mustered out of service because of disability on June 12, 1862. He died in April 1886.

William's son James G. Cross enlisted at age twenty-one on August 9, 1862, in Company A of the 148th New York Infantry Volunteers. He was captured on June 15, 1864, near Petersburg, Virginia. He was sent to the infamous Andersonville prison camp in Georgia, where he died of scurvy on September 13, 1864. He is buried in the Andersonville National Cemetery. He also has a gravestone in Restvale Cemetery in Seneca Falls.

Lemuel B. Cross enlisted at age twenty-three on August 12, 1862. He was mustered in as a member of Company A of the 148th New York Volunteers Infantry on September 14, 1862. (This Company A was known as the Lieutenant Horace N. Rumsey Company A.) The 1860 U.S. census shows that he was a machinist living at 20 Green Street in Seneca Falls with his wife, Margaret. Other records indicate that he was a blacksmith. He suffered a gunshot wound to the left thigh in action at Cold Harbor, Virginia, on June 3, 1864. He was treated at the Base Hospital in White House, Virginia. On June 6, he was transferred by steamboat to the Campbell General Hospital in Washington, D.C. He was transferred back to duty on June 7. The wound never fully healed prior to his discharge. He was mustered out of service on June 22, 1865. After the Civil War, he was a machinist for many years in the pump factories in Seneca Falls. For several years, he and two sons operated a sawing and machining business known as L.B. Cross and Sons on West Bayard Street in Seneca Falls. He is believed to have purchased the first horseless carriage in Seneca Falls. He and his wife, Margaret, had

Lemuel Cross was wounded at Cold Harbor on June 3, 1864. The GAR post in Seneca Falls was named in honor of Lemuel Cross, four of his brothers and his father, all of whom served in the Civil War. *Seneca Falls Historical Society*.

three sons and two daughters. He lived the last six years of his life with his daughter in Syracuse. He died on August 26, 1927.

Eighteen-year-old George M. Cross enlisted on April 30, 1863, as a member of Company D of the Eleventh New York Heavy Artillery. This company was consolidated with Company M of the Fourth New York Heavy Artillery at the battle at Gettysburg. He was one of many Union soldiers who were moved into the New York City area during the famous draft riots taking place shortly after the conclusion of the Gettysburg battle. He suffered a wound to his right index finger while on duty at Fort Richmond in New York Harbor on July 15, 1863. He suffered a gunshot wound to the left arm on April 2, 1865, at the Battle of Boynton Plank Road (Sutherland Station). He was mustered out for disability on July 25, 1865, at Harewood Hospital in Washington, D.C. In 1867, he moved to Owendale in Brookfield Township, Michigan, where he was a farmer and carpenter. He was injured in a barn raising in 1912 and died on July 26, 1913.

William's son Asa D. Cross enlisted at age twenty-eight on June 6, 1863, in Company M of the Fourth New York Artillery. He was listed as "missing" when his unit was mustered out of service on September 26, 1865. Perhaps that helps to explain why there were reports that he had died as a prisoner at Andersonville. Records clearly indicate, however, that he returned to Seneca Falls after the war and was admitted to the Utica/Rome Asylum and that his father reimbursed Seneca County $100 for Asa's care there. He died in Seneca Falls and is buried in Restvale Cemetery.

William H. and Lucy Cross had younger sons (William H. Jr., Norman and Charles) who were too young to serve in the war.

The GAR post #78 established in Seneca Falls, New York, was named in honor of the Cross men.[81] For many years, that post had over four hundred members and was active in the observance of Memorial Day and many other social functions throughout the year. By 1931, the post had only three surviving members: William T. Smith, John Hier and William H. Beach.[82]

MARY GAHAN, VETERAN OF THE 148TH

Mary Gahan was a laundress in the 148th New York Infantry during the Civil War. She joined when her husband, Jeremiah "Jerry" Gahan, enlisted on August 28, 1862, in Company H, and she stayed with the regiment until it mustered out in 1865. Jerry Gahan was an "average soldier" who did his job and was never wounded, promoted or disciplined.[83]

Mary's job was to launder and mend soldiers' clothing. She received a fee for doing this work and traveled with the regiment. One person described her efforts this way: "In all the marches of that regiment Mary bore her part as bravely as the strongest soldier of them all. She shared the perils and fatigues of its Virginia Campaigns and was with it at its triumphant return."[84]

Gravestone of Mary Gahan, who went along with her husband when he served in the 148th New York Volunteers. *Caren Cleaveland.*

Following the Civil War, Mary and Jerry Gahan lived in Waterloo, New York. Mary was always present at the regimental reunions, "and the boys will remember the hearty emphasis of her assertions on such occasions that she 'belonged to the 148th.'"[85]

She died of heart disease on July 4, 1881, at the age of forty-nine. Her funeral took place at the St. Mary's Church in Waterloo. The bearers were all veterans of the 148th, and her coffin was draped with the regimental colors.[86] She is buried in St. Mary's Cemetery in Waterloo.[87]

The July 15, 1881 *Phelps Advertiser* noted of Mary: "Her kindness of heart and cheery disposition will cause her to be long remembered by the survivors of the 148th, and her death will be regretted in no less degree than that of the other comrades who have gone before; whose names are now inscribed on the last great muster roll."[88]

The Blew Brothers of Sheldrake

John Stout Blew and Ann M. Tibbits Blew of Sheldrake had twenty-two children, of which eighteen survived at least into their teens. Two of their sons, Samuel and Oscar, served in Company C of the 126th New York Volunteers and died during the Civil War.

Samuel Blew was born on February 7, 1840, the tenth child. At the age of twenty-two, he enlisted on August 5, 1862, in Captain Winfield Scott's Company C of the 126th New York Volunteers. He fought in the Harpers Ferry battle in mid-September 1862 and was killed at Gettysburg on July 3, 1863. He was twenty-three years, four months and twenty-one days old at the time.

Oscar Ditmars Blew was born on February 3, 1841, the eleventh child. Like his brother Samuel, he enlisted in Captain Winfield Scott's Company C of the 126th New York Volunteers on August 15, 1862. He was one of the many members of the 126th who surrendered at the Battle of Harpers Ferry on September 15, 1862. Although sick, he was taken to the Camp Douglas prison camp in Illinois. He died there on October 26, 1862. He was twenty-one years, eight months and twenty-three days old at the time. The names of both Samuel and Oscar appear on the same headstone in the Fairview Cemetery in Sheldrake.

There are two confusing issues regarding the history of this family. One is the spelling of the last name. In 1807, Samuel and Rebecca Blue left New

Jersey and settled on Military Lot 14 of Ovid Township. They had bought two hundred acres to the south of the Sheldrake crossroads. They had two children: Sally and John Stout. After John Stout Blue's death in 1854, some of his sons apparently changed the family name to Blew. There is some speculation that they felt that spelling was better than that of the color. That helps to explain why in the draft book *Civil War Soldiers of Seneca County, New York*, former Seneca County Historian Betty Auten used the "Blue" spelling rather than "Blew."

Another confusing matter arises from the death of George Blue on September 12, 1863. Some reports state that he died as a soldier in the Civil War like his brothers Samuel and Oscar. No evidence has been uncovered to verify these reports. Perhaps the confusion arises simply from the fact that he died a few weeks after the Battle of Gettysburg.

Whether it is two or three sons who died in actual service in the Union army in the Civil War, it is true that in the span of less than a year, Ann Blew suffered the loss of three sons. She had been widowed since her husband's death in 1854, leaving her to oversee a large family and farm. Undoubtedly the loss of those three sons made the situation that much more difficult.[89]

THE VAN SICKLE BROTHERS OF SHELDRAKE

Four sons of Annon and Ann Tillyer Van Sickle of Sheldrake served in the Union army. The first one to enlist was David Van Sickle, who was the fifth child. He enlisted in Company G of the Fifteenth New York Infantry on October 30, 1861. He was involved in battles at Chattanooga, Shiloh, Chickamauga and Mission Ridge and was discharged on October 21, 1864. He and his wife, Celestia Emmons, had five children. He lived in the Sheldrake area the rest of his life and is buried in Lake View Cemetery in Interlaken.

William Van Sickle, the fourth child, enlisted in Company E of the 148th New York Volunteers on August 31, 1862. He was engaged in battles at Petersburg, Cold Harbor and Drury's Bluff. He was wounded on June 18, 1864, near Petersburg, Virginia, and was discharged for disability on April 3, 1865. He was a hotel keeper in Geneva at the time of his marriage to Nancy M. Kinne on June 25, 1884.

Milton Van Sickle was the sixth child in the family. He is believed to be buried at the Andersonville prison cemetery. There is a monument to him in the Fairview Cemetery in Sheldrake.

Eighth child John Van Sickle enlisted on August 5, 1864, in Company B of the Third New York Artillery. He was involved in battles at James Island and Monk Corner. He was discharged on July 13, 1865. After the war, he and his wife, Ann, lived in Ovid, where he was a stonemason.

Annon and Ann Van Sickle had four other children—three daughters and one son—who were much too young for military service during the Civil War.[90]

JOHN THOMAS MAYNARD OF JUNIUS

John Thomas Maynard was born in Junius on October 6, 1843, the son of John P. and Salinda Steward Maynard. He was employed as a clerk prior to this enlistment at the age of nineteen on August 8, 1862, in Company B of the 126th New York Infantry. He was involved in the Battle of Harpers Ferry and later served in the ambulance corps. He was discharged with other members of his company on June 3, 1865, near Alexandria, Virginia. He died on January 7, 1866, at the age of twenty-two and is buried alongside his parents in the Quaker Cemetery on Nine Foot Road in Waterloo.[91]

John Thomas Maynard of Junius died about six months after his discharge from military service. *Waterloo Historical Society*.

The McDuffees of Varick

There were three McDuffee brothers and three of their relatives—all from the town of Varick—who served in the Union army in the Civil War.

The three brothers were Robert, Darwin and Stinson, who were the sons of Nelson and Nancy McDuffee. Robert, age twenty-six, and Darwin, age twenty, both enlisted on August 30, 1862, in Company E of the Forty-fourth New York Infantry. The 1860 U.S. census listed Robert as a wagonmaker and living with his wife, Emma. Robert was wounded and captured on May 8, 1864, at Laurel Hill, Virginia. On June 15, 1864, he died of his wounds while a prisoner of war at Richmond.

Darwin was discharged for disability on February 2, 1863, in Baltimore, Maryland. The 1880 U.S. census listed him as an employee of a shoemaker and living in the town of Covert with wife, Martha, and daughters, Minnie and Lottie. In 1895, he had a new wife, Elizabeth. He died on May 11, 1919, in the Ithaca Hospital, having been hospitalized because of a fall. He is buried in the Lake View Cemetery in Interlaken.

Brother Stinson enlisted on December 26, 1863, as a private in Company D of the 148th New York Volunteers. He was later transferred to the 100th New York Infantry. He was discharged from military service on August 28, 1865, at Richmond, Virginia. Prior to his enlistment, he was a cooper. Following the war, he continued to live in Varick in the small hamlet called McDuffietown. (Note the difference in spelling between his last name and the name of the hamlet.) He married Salina Odell of Canoga, and they had two children: Bert and Gertrude. Stinson died on May 21, 1925. He is buried in the Oak Hill Cemetery in McDuffietown.

Warren McDuffee enlisted on August 25, 1862, at age eighteen as a private in Company D of the 148th New York Infantry. His parents were William, who had died on May 17, 1861, and Charity. Warren was killed in battle near Petersburg, Virginia, on June 18, 1864. He was buried on the battlefield.

Hamilton McDuffee enlisted at age eighteen on August 29, 1862, in Company D of the 148th New York Infantry. He was the son of Palmer and Elizabeth Jane McDuffee. Hamilton's father had died in 1859. Hamilton was shot in the thigh on October 7, 1864, at Fort Harrison, Virginia. He was discharged with his detachment on June 4, 1865, at Petersburg. Following the Civil War, the family moved to Seneca Falls, where Hamilton was a shipping clerk at the woolen mill. His wife, Jennie, died in 1892. At the time of his death on February 19, 1910, Hamilton was living at the home of his only daughter, Josephine (Mrs. Arthur) Littlejohn. He is buried in the Restvale Cemetery in Seneca Falls. His mother died on September 11, 1925.

Cyrus F. McDuffee enlisted at age twenty on August 30, 1862, in Company E of the 44th New York Infantry. He was wounded in April 1864. In October 1864, he was transferred to Company E of the 140th New York Volunteers. He was discharged on June 4, 1865, near Alexandria, Virginia. He married Kate M. Swartz of Seneca Falls on November 17, 1866. He married Anna M. Hubbard on October 2, 1873. The 1880 U.S. census listed Cyrus as living in Oneida and working as a carpenter.[92]

DAVID GENOA CAYWOOD OF OVID

David Genoa Caywood was both a prisoner and wounded in his first enlistment but served a second enlistment as well. *Wayne E. Morrison Jr.*

The only Seneca County chapter of the Sons of Union Veterans is officially named the David G. Caywood Camp #146. It is named in honor of David Genoa Caywood, who was a native of Ovid. The Ovid-area GAR Post #435 had also been named in his honor.

David Caywood was born on July 2, 1839, in Ovid. After attending the Ovid Academy, he studied law in the office of John E. Seeley. On September 30, 1861, he enlisted in Company J of the Thirty-third New York Regiment. He was wounded at Fredericksburg, Virginia, on May 4, 1862. He was captured and taken to Libby Prison in Richmond and exchanged on May 18, 1862. He went back into service with his regiment and was wounded in his right side and discharged on June 6, 1862. On August 30, 1862, he enlisted for three years in Company H of the Thirty-third New York Regiment and was promoted to the rank of corporal on

October 1. He was mustered in as a second lieutenant in Company I on April 30, 1862.

At the end of the Civil War, Caywood practiced law briefly and moved to New York City in 1867. He served for two years as a sergeant in the city police force. He resigned from that position to serve in the sub-treasury in New York. In 1885, he retired after seventeen years in that position and then became involved in the insurance business. He died on February 10, 1890, in New York City. He was survived by his wife, Ellen; sons David and William; and daughters Clara, Nellie and Mary. He is buried in Ovid Union Cemetery.[93]

Andrew J. Chestnut

The Lodi post of the GAR, Post No. 445, chartered on January 24, 1884, was named for Andrew J. Chestnut. Chestnut had enlisted at age twenty-three on August 22, 1862, as a private in the 126th New York Infantry. At the time of his enlistment, he was a farmer in Lodi. He fought at Harpers Ferry, Gettysburg and in several battles in Virginia. He was promoted to corporal. He was killed in action at Morton's Ford, Virginia, on February 6, 1864. He is buried in the West Lodi Cemetery, where his tombstone bears the following epitaph: "Angels bear him safely upward; Place his head on Jesus' breast; From the field of battle bear him; Up where all is peace and rest."[94]

Andrew Chestnut was born in 1842 in Ireland, the son of Patrick and Margaret Chestnut.[95]

James Souhan of Canoga

At the age of thirty-five, James Souhan of Canoga enlisted on December 23, 1863, as a private in Company C of the Nineteenth New York Heavy Artillery. He was discharged on August 21, 1865. What is particularly noteworthy about Souhan is the fact that he became a naturalized U.S. citizen shortly after his discharge from military service and the way in which his wife, Ann, earned money to support the family while James was in the

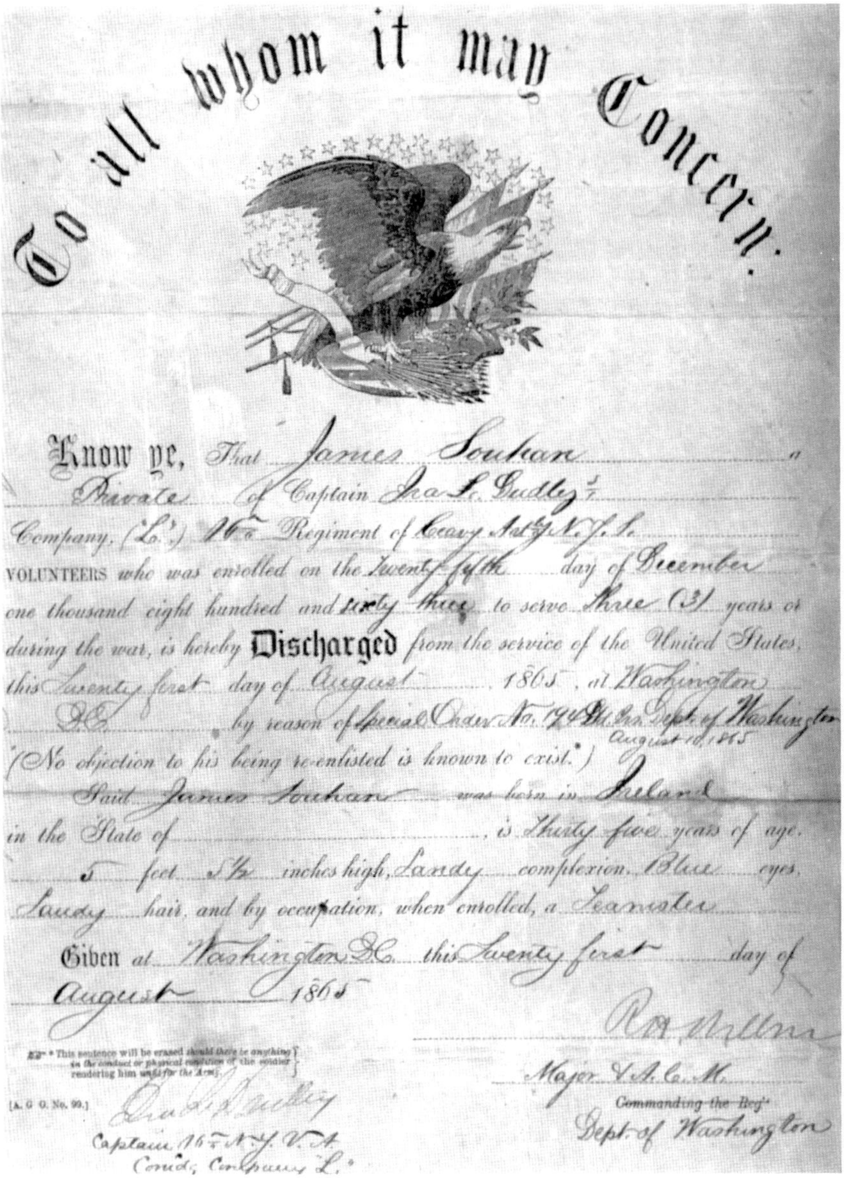

To all whom it may Concern:

Know ye, That James Souhan a Private of Captain Ira L. Dudley's Company, (L) 16th Regiment of Heavy Art'y N.Y.S. VOLUNTEERS who was enrolled on the twenty fifth day of December one thousand eight hundred and sixty three to serve three (3) years or during the war, is hereby Discharged from the service of the United States, this twenty first day of August, 1865, at Washington D.C. by reason of Special Order No. 194 Hd Qrs Dept of Washington August 10, 1865

(*No objection to his being re-enlisted is known to exist.*)

Said James Souhan was born in Ireland in the State of ______, is thirty five years of age, 5 feet 5½ inches high, Sandy complexion, Blue eyes, Sandy hair, and by occupation, when enrolled, a Teamster.

Given at Washington D.C. this twenty first day of August 1865

R A Allen
Major & A.A.G.M.
~~Commanding the Reg't~~
Dept of Washington

*This sentence will be erased should there be anything in the conduct or physical condition of the soldier rendering him unfit for the Army.

[A. G. O. No. 99.]

Ira L. Dudley
Captain 16th N.Y.V.A.
Comd'g Company L.

Discharge papers for James Souhan, an Irish immigrant who served in the Nineteenth New York Heavy Artillery. *The Souhan family.*

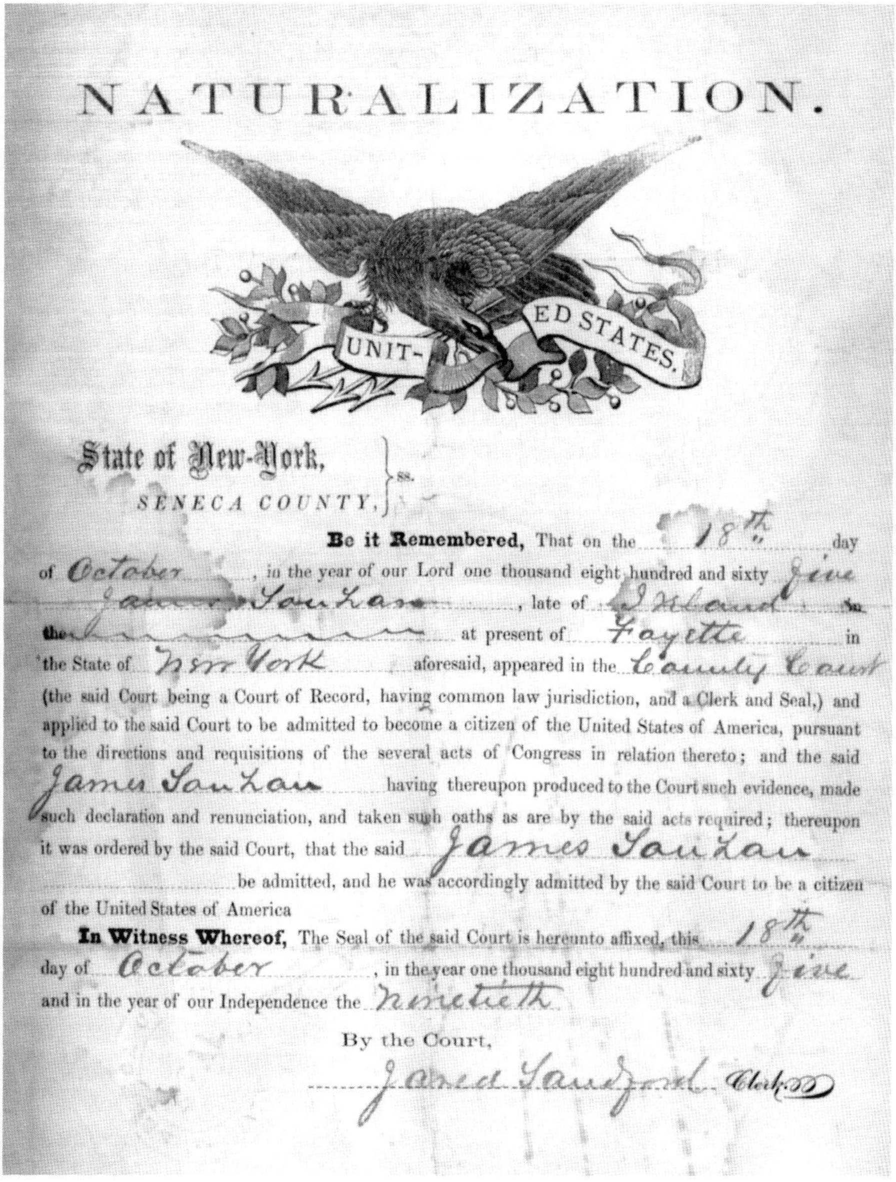

NATURALIZATION.

UNIT-ED STATES.

State of New-York, } ss.
SENECA COUNTY,

Be it Remembered, That on the 18th day of October, in the year of our Lord one thousand eight hundred and sixty five James Souhan, late of Ireland in the [illegible] at present of Fayette in the State of New York aforesaid, appeared in the County Court (the said Court being a Court of Record, having common law jurisdiction, and a Clerk and Seal,) and applied to the said Court to be admitted to become a citizen of the United States of America, pursuant to the directions and requisitions of the several acts of Congress in relation thereto; and the said James Souhan having thereupon produced to the Court such evidence, made such declaration and renunciation, and taken such oaths as are by the said acts required; thereupon it was ordered by the said Court, that the said James Souhan be admitted, and he was accordingly admitted by the said Court to be a citizen of the United States of America

In Witness Whereof, The Seal of the said Court is hereunto affixed, this 18th day of October, in the year one thousand eight hundred and sixty five and in the year of our Independence the ninetieth.

By the Court,

Jared Sandford Clerk.

James Souhan became a naturalized U.S. citizen after the Civil War. *The Souhan family.*

service. James Souhan was born in Dublin, Ireland, and came to the United States with a brother in the late 1850s. He married Ann Honor Caveny on June 8, 1861. Prior to James's enlistment, the couple had a son, James, and Ann was pregnant with a daughter, Mary, who was born in 1864. While James was in the service, Ann continued to live in Canoga. She would walk about nine miles from Canoga to Seneca Falls to pick up work from one of the several mills, piece work that she carried home and finished and then carried back to the mill. Following the war, James and Ann had two more daughters. James died in 1885 and is buried in the old Catholic portion of Restvale Cemetery in Seneca Falls. Ann received a widow's pension starting in 1886.[96]

JOHN M. HILL: SENECA COUNTY'S LAST SURVIVING CIVIL WAR VETERAN

At the time of his death on August 22, 1940, John M. Hill was the last surviving Civil War veteran from Seneca County. He was also the last commander of the Tyler J. Snyder Post, GAR, in Waterloo.

John was born in Junius on May 19, 1846, the son of Abram and Nancy Hill. When he was sixteen, he tried to enlist in the Union army but was stopped by his father. He waited a year and enlisted in Battery B of the Third New York Light Artillery. Most of his military service was in various campaigns in the Carolinas, where he served as a driver of a lead team. At the time of his ninety-fourth birthday, he was quoted in a local newspaper as saying, "I came out without a scratch, but I lost one of my closest friends and comrades in the battle of Honey Hill. There was only one time during the war that I wished I had not enlisted, and that was my first night in camp at Fortress Monroe. I guess it was homesickness, but it didn't last long."[97]

He was discharged on September 7, 1864, at Syracuse, New York, because of rheumatism.

John M. Hill worked as a carpenter until 1930. He married Mary Jane Buck on October 15, 1868, and they had four children, three of whom lived into adulthood. Daughter Charlotte (Lottie) was born on October 12, 1891, and married Peter Doran. Daughter Ella Elizabeth married Richard Brophy. Son Frank married Harriet Hayes. The John M. Hill family lived at 30 Center Street in Waterloo. Following his wife's death,

John M. Hill of Waterloo was the last surviving Seneca County veteran of the Civil War. He died in 1940. *Waterloo Historical Society.*

John lived with his daughter Charlotte. John is buried in Maple Grove Cemetery in Waterloo.[98]

At the time of his ninety-fourth birthday party, John Hill was asked if he would again enlist, knowing now what that would mean. His bowed shoulders straightened up, a glint came into his eyes and he said, "Yes sir—if America was threatened by foreign soldiers."[99]

Chapter 9

JOHN L. HOSTER: ADVENTURES OF A CIVIL WAR SOLDIER

John Loudebank Hoster, my great-grandfather, spent most of his life in the Canoga area of the town of Fayette. He was born on July 15, 1842, and died on October 30, 1930. He survived his ordeals of the Confederate prison camps at Andersonville, Georgia, and Florence, South Carolina. In his postwar life, he operated a sawmill and a cider press.

This is one of two daguerreotypes taken of John L. Hoster while he was stationed in the Suffolk, Virginia area. *Walter Gable.*

John L. Hoster dressed in a suit shortly before he entered military service. *New York State Historical Association.*

We know so much about his Civil War service because he kept very detailed journal entries throughout his military service. What he recorded in terms of his daily food intake as a prisoner has been widely used by Civil War scholars to document what may well have been the typical privations of prisoners at Andersonville and Florence. The account of his Civil War service serves as a case study to help us understand the day-to-day experiences of many "average" soldiers. As much as possible, this chapter uses Hoster's actual wording from his diary entries.

Enlistment in the 148th New York Volunteers Regiment

John L. Hoster enlisted on August 11, 1862, in Company A of the 148th New York Volunteers. He was at least partially motivated by patriotism, as shown in his diary entry for September 22, 1863. He wrote, "One year ago today I bade adieu to my friends and my native shore and set out with the determination to render all the assistance in my power for the preservation of the Union." He must have been motivated by the economic incentives, but no written evidence of his thoughts on that factor has been found. Abolition of slavery was not one of his primary motivations for enlistment. His diary entries frequently suggest a racist attitude, common for many Union soldiers. For example, his April 12, 1863 diary entry includes the following: "...Every African that attempts to pass by is quickly summoned to the rifle pit, by the following kind words, 'Come in here you damn nigger,' where the sable African is furnished with a shovel, which some Co. A boy has not the energy enough to handle."

In Company A, he found himself surrounded by his friends and neighbors from Seneca Falls, Fayette, Canoga and Geneva. The regiment received approximately a month's training at Camp Swift in Geneva. On September 22, 1862, along with the other members of the various companies of 148th New York Volunteers, he left Geneva for the rendezvous camp at Elmira, traveling by boat down Seneca Lake to Jefferson (Watkins Glen) and then by railroad to Elmira.

Initial Active Duty in the Portsmouth/Suffolk, Virginia Area

From October 11, 1862, to early May 1864, Hoster was assigned to the greater Portsmouth/Suffolk area, establishing Camp Folger and doing supply and guard duty. His specific work consisted primarily of picket and guard duty (earning him a promotion to sergeant of the guard) and assisting the captain in preparing the payrolls and ordering supplies. Frequently he was the messenger who went to the commissary to get clothing and other items.

Until spring 1864, Hoster was not engaged in combat. His actual duty gave him a great deal of free time. On several occasions, he was able to secure a pass so that he could visit the cities of Portsmouth and Norfolk. Having come from a very rural area, it must have been quite an experience for him to see "city life" so frequently. On a few occasions, he went to the theater, seeing performances by such great actors and singers of the time as the Webb sisters and Jenny Lind. He also had ample time to read and write.[100]

Several diary entries, such as "rained all day" or "stormed all day, part rain and part snow—rather cold tonight," suggest that enduring the weather in tents was not desirable.

In his November 24 entry, he wrote about a newly established schedule:

6:30—Reveille
7:00—Breakfast
7:30—Surgeons Call
8:00—Guard Mounting
9:00—Inspection Arms
10:00—Company Drill
11:00—Recall
12:00—Dinner
2:00—Battalion Drill
3:30—Recall
4:00—Dress Parade
Sundown—Retreat
8:00—Tattoo
9:00—Taps

On Sunday, May 24, 1863, Hoster attended a service at the Baptist church. He recorded, "…heard a fine sermon by a Secesh preacher. He did not say anything out of the way [meaning that the Southern pastor didn't say anything negative about the Union]."

Infectious diseases could spread easily, considering the conditions under which the soldiers had to work. Hoster had a bout with measles.

On June 16, 1863, he wrote, "Do not feel very spruce today. I have a constant irritation in my throat which causes me to cough violently." The next day, he went to the doctor and expected he was coming down with the measles, adding that he had coughed all night until past midnight. The next day (Thursday, June 18, 1863), he went to the doctor again and wrote, "My cough is as bad as ever." On June 19, he wrote that he was still on the sick list. On the twentieth, he wrote, "…measles still making their appearance." His only writing for June 21 was, "Sick enough to die without kicking." The next day, he simply wrote, "Sick as blazes." On the twenty-third, he wrote, "Can eat a little soup today." It is not until Monday, June 29, that he wrote, "Feeling very well considering, but have to stay in my quarters. Am very weak." Finally, on July 1, he wrote, "I am feeling first rate today."

Hoster's First Battle Engagements and His Capture

It was on May 4, 1864, that John L. Hoster and the other 148th New York Volunteers left the Williamsburg, Virginia area to participate for the first time in the fighting on the Virginia battlefront. He was part of the assault on the Confederate lines at Cold Harbor in early June 1864, during which the Union suffered huge losses in killed and wounded.

On Wednesday, June 15, Hoster was taken prisoner. The following is most of his diary entry for that day:

> *We started out very early this morning, crossing the Appomattox on a pontoon bridge…There was any amount of cherries there, but we could not get a chance to eat any. We proceeded a short distance when nearly all of our regt. was sent on skirmish, the right of our company on the Appomattox. We ran into the enemy skirmish line before we were aware of it. They fired a volley into us. We concealed ourselves as much as possible and during the day we dug small rifle pits for protection. Soon after noon I fired at a man across the river who was taking observations with a glass. He ducked his head and went off around a hill and a battery soon made its appearance and began to throw shot and shell at us, wounding James Roe and Chas. Marshall, H. Co. Benjamin Watkins in*

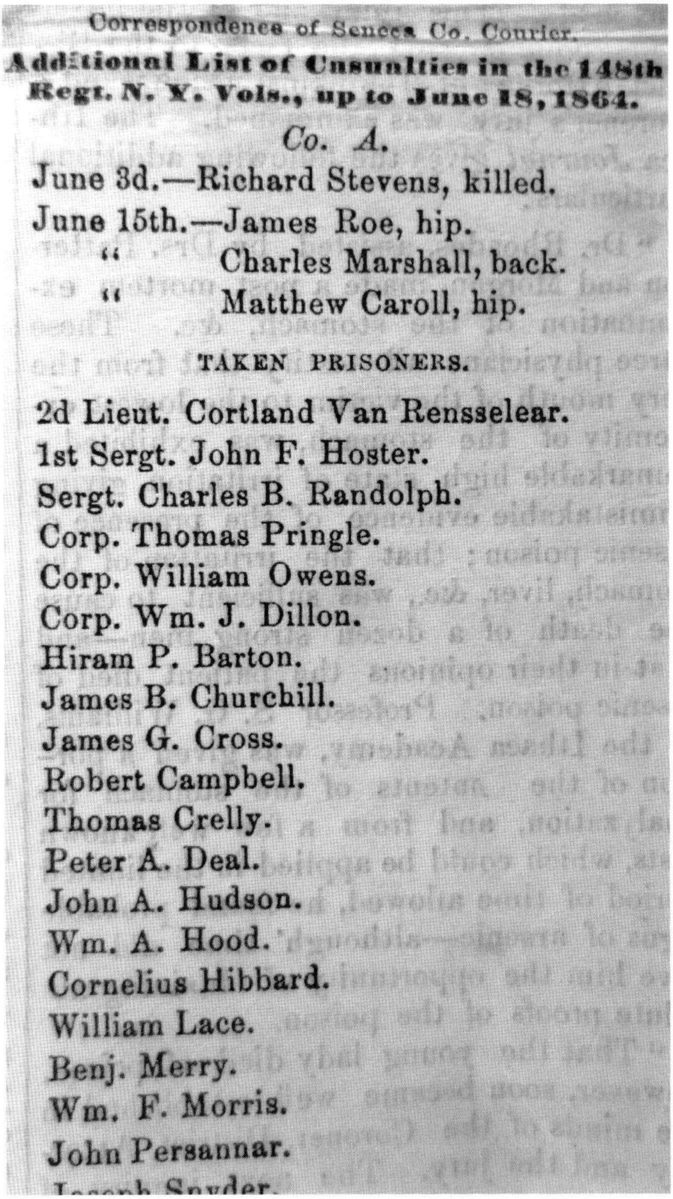

Correspondence of Seneca Co. Courier.

Additional List of Casualties in the 148th Regt. N. Y. Vols., up to June 18, 1864.

Co. A.

June 3d.—Richard Stevens, killed.
June 15th.—James Roe, hip.
" Charles Marshall, back.
" Matthew Caroll, hip.

TAKEN PRISONERS.

2d Lieut. Cortland Van Rensselear.
1st Sergt. John F. Hoster.
Sergt. Charles B. Randolph.
Corp. Thomas Pringle.
Corp. William Owens.
Corp. Wm. J. Dillon.
Hiram P. Barton.
James B. Churchill.
James G. Cross.
Robert Campbell.
Thomas Crelly.
Peter A. Deal.
John A. Hudson.
Wm. A. Hood.
Cornelius Hibbard.
William Lace.
Benj. Merry.
Wm. F. Morris.
John Persannar.
Joseph Snyder.

The *Seneca County Courier* notice of the capture of John L. Hoster and others in his company. *Newspaper clippings compiled by Roberta Halden.*

command on our right fell back offering the rebs an opportunity to flank us. At 4:30 we were obliged to surrender to a company of the 26th Va. We were marched back to their breastworks and sent by the Major in command to the Col. commanding Battery 5. From there to Gen. Wise and to the Custom House in Petersburg where we were questioned, then to P.M. office where we were searched and relieved of our watches, letter knives, etc. My spy glasses were also taken. We were then confined to a building on a back street. There we found Thos. Crelly of our company, who had arrived before us.

A June 17, 1864 letter from Chaplain Ferris Scott to his brother provided more information about how Hoster and his fellow soldiers had to surrender and be taken as prisoner:

But the saddest part of the tale for Seneca Falls remains yet to be told. Lieut. Court. Van Renssalear, as brave and fine an officer as we have in the Regiment, had the misfortune of being captured by the Rebs, together with some 25 or 30 of his Company. He and those captured with him were on the extreme right of the Regiment and had taken possession of a house as a shelter from which to set as sharp shooters. While in the house the Regiment was ordered to fall back. He did not get the order, and was left behind; and before he was aware of it, the Rebs surrounded the house and took the whole squad prisoners. I haven't been able to obtain an accurate list of those taken yet…Sergt. Hoster, John Hudson, and in fact the majority of the good fighting men in the Co., are gone to Richmond. The only ones who escaped were those who had been sent to the rear for ammunition, water, etc. and who were not in the fight at the time.

Hoster and the others captured with him were taken by boxcars on railroad trains to the famous Confederate prison camp in Andersonville, Georgia. Of the over 150 places that were used by either the Union or the Confederacy as prisons during the Civil War, Andersonville is the most infamous. Of the over forty thousand prisoners who were kept there at some point during 1864, nearly thirteen thousand died.

His First Impressions of the Andersonville Prison Camp

Having arrived at the Andersonville prison camp late at night on Sunday, June 19, 1864, it wasn't until the next day that Hoster could really see the conditions of the camp. Following is his June 20 diary entry:

> *Warm, rainy in the afternoon. We are quite comfortable in our tents. I took a stroll through camp today and "Oh! horrors-of-horrors," the sight which greeted my eyes! Some men, not a shred of clothing, others with scarcely a thread to cover their nakedness, others with a shirt and a pair of drawers as black as the ace of spades with grease and dirt. Some have no means of shielding themselves from the inclemency of the weather. Some have a sort of tent made of a woolen blanket and a few have shelter tents. A creek runs through the center of the yard at the*

This is the reconstructed entry gate through which John L. Hoster and other prisoners would have entered Andersonville prison. *Walter Gable.*

The Andersonville prison camp site as it looks today. Only a portion of one corner of the stockade wall and the entrance gate for prisoners have been reconstructed. *Walter Gable.*

lower end of which is a large sink. Nothing but a frame work. Some of the men are not able to go to the sink and do their business just outside their tents in small holes and some have been seen to do it in small holes made with the heel inside the tent, while some do it on the surface outside. Hundreds use the banks of the stream, creating an awful stench and rendering the water unfit to wash in. Thus the slovenly made it unhealthy for us all. The yard covers about 11 acres and contains 25,000 men. The scurvy and dysentery prevail to great extent and the mortality per day averages at least 33 deaths. Rumored that 134 died today. The scurvy seems to be worse among the Belle Isle and Libby prisoners. We drew rations of bread and meat this evening. The meat ration is small, but the bread will do. Some of the men draw their meat raw and cook it to suit themselves.

WHAT THE PRISONERS HAD TO EAT

The prisoners were not provided with adequate food rations in terms of quantity or quality, so it is not surprising that so many of them starved to death or died of scurvy and other diseases. In his June 21, 1864 entry, Hoster wrote, "We had pork and beans for dinner—the pork I had, the beans we bought." The next day, he wrote, "...Bean soup for dinner. We had mush today drawn last night. It was poorly seasoned with salt. We had our last cup of Uncle Sam's coffee for some time this morning." On June 27, he wrote:

> *The mush we drew last night was not cooked at all. We made a sort of gruel of the remainder this morning. I boiled some mush with an old pork bone that I had left in my haversack for my dinner. The bread we drew this evening was but half-baked and sour at that. I ate the whole of it for supper to prevent its getting worse, although it nearly gagged me.*

Hoster must have been one of the more fortunate prisoners in that he managed to survive. In his July 2 diary entry, he wrote, "This afternoon I purchased a small bucket for $1.00 greenback...I cut a strap out of an old boat [note: transcript says "boat" but probably should be "boot"] thereby getting an interest in a well for the three of us. The water is nice and cool and the well is near our tent."

Given the general shortages of food, it should not be surprising that several of the prisoners resorted to stealing whatever they could from their fellow prisoners. Those who were stealing became known as "the Raiders." A group known as "the Regulators" was organized to round up suspected raiders and subject them to a court-martial trial. In his July 11 diary entry, Hoster wrote about six of the raiders who were hanged for their actions. Following is a portion of that entry:

Opposite, top: There was only one small stream that flowed through the Andersonville prison camp. *Walter Gable.*

Opposite, bottom: Reconstructed "shebang" shelters, dead line railing and portion of a reconstructed stockade wall. *Walter Gable.*

> *These were the ringleaders of a large band of raiders...that were the terror of the camp, so bold had they become that it was a common thing for them to knock a man down and rifle his pockets in broad daylight...At precisely 5 P.M. the drop* [the trap door beneath the six men to be hanged] *fell, Mosby's* [he was one of the six] *rope broke and he fell to the ground. Curtis fell farther than the rest and died very soon. Mosby when he fell begged for some of his friends to come forward and rescue him. He offered Limber Jim* [leader of the Regulators] *$1000 to save his life. Limber Jim replied, "You followed me for my money, I'm now following you for your life." He then took him up on the scaffold, adjusted the rope and hood—then jerked the scaffold from under him...*

THE ROLE OF RELIGION IN SURVIVING

Prior to his enlistment, John Hoster, with his parents and siblings, attended Sunday church services regularly. He often—but not every Sunday—attended church services while on military duty in the Suffolk, Virginia area. At Andersonville, however, religion seemed to take on a much greater importance to both him and many of the other prisoners. In his Sunday, July 17, 1864 diary entry, he wrote:

> *This evening quite a congregation formed in from Sergt. Pope's tent and Brother Shephard delivered a discourse from Paul's first letter to Timothy—6th Chapter, 12th verse. The discourse was very interesting. Preachings and prayer meetings have been held during the past week and I learn that several have committed their souls to God. God's Holy Spirit can find the heart of the persistant* [sic] *even in this loathsome place.*

In several subsequent diary entries, Hoster made reference to his spending time reading the New Testament and that the evening prayer group was meeting.

Death an Ever-Present Reality

Given that about one in three prisoners at Andersonville died there, Hoster had to endure death as an ever-present reality. He was particularly disturbed by the death of a young prisoner who had been a soldier in the Nineteenth Massachusetts Volunteers. In his diary for July 17, 1864, Hoster wrote:

> *Redford Davinee, a boy of 17 yrs. of age and a member of G. Co., 19th Mass. Vol., died this afternoon near our tent. Disease, dysentery and rheumatism—the boy has no mother and was living with his sisters previous to his enlisting in April last... When we first saw him he was a perfect picture of despair—his countenance wore a sad expression and that dread disease, homesickness, was fast wearing his life away. We fixed up his blanket for him and nursed him as best as we could till Death came to his relief. Thus hundreds die by being exposed to the burning rays of the Georgia sun with no one to cheer up their downcast spirits.*

An especially great loss was the death of his tentmate Tom on Sunday, September 4. For several days Hoster had been telling about Tom's being sick and getting sicker. On September 3, he wrote, "Tom has been delirious all day, talking about his mother and sisters being here and asking me whether my father and mother had been here. He also said his brother John had been here and left him some money and he could not find it." On the day Tom died, Hoster wrote, "Tom died this evening just after dark. He died very easy. Once during the day he seemed quite conscious for a few moments and uttered quite an audible prayer." The following day, Hoster wrote:

> *After roll call, Lace, Morris, Personnar and myself carried Tom out to the dead house...After we came back, Personnar and I took two rubber blankets, Tom's shirt and a pair of socks and started for the creek. I washed the shirt and socks thoroughly as I intend to wear them. I changed shirts with Tom. This afternoon I procured a shovel, took off the top course in the tent, and policed around it, putting a quantity of sand on the bottom and burying the filth.*

The next day, he wrote that he went to the creek and gave "my shirt" another washing.

TRANSFER TO THE NEW PRISON CAMP AT FLORENCE, SOUTH CAROLINA

For several days, there were rumors that the Andersonville prisoners were going to be evacuated—before they might be liberated by Union forces. On Thursday, September 8, 1864, Hoster was finally removed from Andersonville. He did not know if he was to be released or simply transferred to another prison camp. He spent some time in the Charleston, South Carolina area. It was after dark on Thursday, October 6, that John L. Hoster and many other prisoners arrived at the Stockade, a brand-new prison camp near Florence, South Carolina.

Between October 1864 and its abandonment in March 1865, the Florence Stockade housed over 15,000 prisoners. Of these, nearly 2,800 died in captivity—some 20 to 30 per day.

Examples of the makeshift "shebang" shelters that provided prisoners at the Florence, South Carolina prison camp with some protection from the harsh summer sun. *Walter Gable.*

Visitor kiosk at the site of the Florence, South Carolina prison camp. *Walter Gable.*

DIET FOR PRISONERS AT THE FLORENCE PRISON CAMP

Food, or the lack of it, was a recurring theme in the various prisoner accounts that survive today. From the very beginning, Confederate officials had expressed concern over their ability to supply adequate rations to the prisoners. Supplying sufficient food for the prisoners became more difficult as time passed and supply lines were cut by the advancing Union troops. The chart below shows what food items John L. Hoster consumed during the month of October 1864.[101]

At Florence, no vegetables other than sweet potatoes were ever issued to the prisoners—except occasionally to hospital inmates.[102] These rations seldom included any meat but rather consisted of "sorghum sirup [*sic*] and meal." The recommended syrup ration was cut to one gill (¼ pint or ½ cup) per

Date	Number of Meals	Rice	Beans	Beef	Flour	Meal	Flour/ Meal	Hominy	Sweet Potato	Molasses	Salt
7	2	X	X		X						
8	2	X	X			X	X				
9	2	X	X		X						X
10	2				X	X				X	
11	1				X						
12	1				X						
13	2		X		X	X		X			
14	2		X				X	X		X	
15	2		X					X			
16	3		X			X	X				
17	3		X			X					
18	1		X	X				X			

Date	Number of Meals	Rice	Beans	Beef	Flour	Meal	Flour/ Meal	Hominy	Sweet Potato	Molasses	Salt
19	ND										
20	2				X		X				
21	2					X				X	
22	2		X		X						
23	1		X			X					
24	2		X			X					
25	1		X			X					
26	0										
27	2						X				
28	1		X		X	X					
29	3		X		X				X		
30	1		X	X	X	X					
31	1		X	X	X						

Reconstruction of the former stockade wall at the Florence, South Carolina prison camp is taking place. *Walter Gable.*

prisoner per day, and eventually even that small amount could not be maintained as time passed and supply lines broke down.

Historical scholars suggest that the journal entries of John L. Hoster provide "the most unbiased view of the diet for prisoners at the stockade that is currently available from any source." But even his journal entries present some problems, as he received extra rations as a member of the Police Club and there are also some gaps in the entries.

Release from the Florence Prison Camp

On Friday, February 17, 1865, Hoster was part of a group of prisoners taken from the Stockade at Florence. Hoster does not indicate that he knew what their destination was. It is possible that he thought they were simply being taken to still another prison camp. In his journal entry for February 20, Hoster mentioned for the first time that he felt he and the others were to be part of a prisoner exchange.

Hoster wrote the following in his journal entry for Sunday, February 26: "Were ordered over the creek where we received a parole according to the cartel of 1-62 to be exchanged in 90 days after date of parole. Went into camp. Prepared to cook, but were ordered to Goldsborough to take the cars. Arrived there some time after dark and boarded the train. Terribly crowded—soon started toward Wilmington." It is significant that Hoster does not suggest any heightened emotions at the prospect of his imminent release from his months of imprisonment. His actual release as a prisoner is recorded in his February 27 journal entry:

> *Ran last night within 30 miles of our lines and halted till morning when we again started on. Arrived at point of exchange quite early. Were counted by Yank and Rebel officers. Feeling indescribable on entering our lines. Marched about a mile to camp. Received rations of whiskey immediately, afterwards coffee, hardtack and fresh beef. Lt. Clough came round and took Owens, Peterson and me to his headquarters and gave us a dinner of hardtack, pork, cornbread and tea. Had good wash before dinner. For supper, hardtack, pork, cornbread, stewed dried apples, tea and coffee. Sat up till late and chatted with Clough. Had good smoke. Clough filled our haversacks with sugar, hardtack, tea and pork.*

Hoster's saying that he was "feeling indescribable on entering our lines" is a highly emotional contrast to the lack of emotion in his journal entry for the previous day. It is interesting to note that his "good wash" might well have been his first good body cleaning in some time and that he so enjoyed a "good smoke." His comments help us to understand just how good life was in the Union camps in the last months of the war compared to Hoster's mere "fight for existence" in the prison camp at Florence.

The next day, Hoster and his associates got to Wilmington. On March 1, they got on a "transport" ship that started down the channel to Savannah. His journal entries make it clear that he didn't sleep much the four nights it took to reach Savannah—because of lice. On Sunday, March 5, they reached Annapolis. There, he bought some clothing items and continued to eat big meals. He might have been released as a prisoner, but the physical toll on his body was still of concern. His journal entry for Wednesday, March 8, noted that he received two months' pay and that "…my feet are so sore, caused, I think, by scurvy."

ARRIVAL HOME

On Friday, March 10, 1865, Hoster wrote, "Received furloughs today [at Baltimore]." The following day, he took the train to Elmira, New York, and then the 6:00 p.m. train to Canandaigua. On late Sunday, March 12, he arrived by train in Seneca Falls, where he spent the night with the Littlejohn family. Hoster assumed that because it was so late at night that his uncle Michael had already gone to bed. His entry for Monday, March 13, includes the following: "I could hardly get through the Falls for the blockade of friends…Our folks were terribly glad to see me. Had a fine supper at home. Lots of friends came to see me. Also in the infantile band from Canoga…"

Although he was adjusting well to his return home, he still had some residual problems. For example, in his Sunday, March 19, journal entry, he included, "I am obliged to sleep every day. I suppose it is caused by weakness." In his March 22 entry, he noted that he then weighed 133.0 pounds, which was 10.5 pounds more than when he had arrived home just a week earlier. There was also the "issue" of his only being home on "furlough." His Saturday, April 1 journal entry stated that he went to Dr. Seely, who "says he will give me a certificate for 20 days more and thinks there will be no danger in staying." He and his friend Charles Peterson got their "certificates" for twenty days on Saturday, April 8. That meant he could continue his furlough and would not have to return to active duty for the remaining few days of the war. Lee surrendered at Appomattox on April 9, essentially bringing the war to an end. Hoster had survived both the Andersonville and Florence prison camps and now had his future ahead.

Part II

THE HOMEFRONT: COPING AND THRIVING

I further proclaim, that if any State shall fail to raise the quota assigned to it by the War Department under this call, then a draft for the deficiency in said quota shall be made on said State.

—President Abraham Lincoln, A Proclamation, October 24, 1863

Chapter 10

THE CIVIL WAR WAS A TREMENDOUS BOOST TO SENECA COUNTY INDUSTRIES AND FARMS

It is commonly said that it was the industrial prowess of the North that enabled the Union to win out over the Confederacy in a prolonged war. Clearly, the Civil War was a financial windfall to many industries and farmers in Seneca County.

Seneca County Wheat Farming During the Civil War

Miss Ethel Buckley, my high school history teacher, would often share tidbits of local history. One of these tidbits that has remained with me all these years is that many of the fine houses on Route 414 between Seneca Falls and Fayette were built by the profits that farmers made selling wheat during the Civil War years. These houses are known locally as the "Wheat Houses of Route 414." I would tell students in my U.S. history courses this same story when we were studying the Civil War period. It is only recently, however, that I have been able to find some real documentation to support what Miss Buckley said. I found this information in reading a 1967 article written by David C. Smith. He based his article on the diaries of Henry K. Dey.

This is a 2014 picture of one of the several "wheat houses" built with the profits made from the soaring wheat prices during the Civil War. *Walter Gable.*

Henry K. Dey operated a 150-acre farm on the eastern shore of Seneca Lake where present-day Sampson State Park is located. Like most area farmers, Dey raised wheat as his basic cash crop. He grew both white (White Flint) and red (Old Red Chief) wheat, as well as some Mediterranean strains. All was winter wheat planted in September, with timothy or clover seed sown on the wheat field in April and the crop harvested in late July.

Although Seneca County wheat farmers were having increasing difficulty competing with the prairie farms of the Great Plains, the Civil War created a great demand for whatever amount of wheat could be produced for market. The *Geneva Courier* carried the following editorial:

> *Farmers—At this crisis in our country's history let not the farmer forget to make ample provisions for food for the thousands now rallying to hold up untarnished and cause forever to float that Star Spangled Banner—the pride of the world...The farmers should double the amount of ground*

> *heretofore used for the various seeds and permit not a foot of soil to become accountless... We entreat every farmer in the town(s) of Seneca and old Ontario to feel that they have an individual responsibility resting upon them.*

The increased demand for wheat during the Civil War years is reflected in its selling price. In 1862, Mr. Dey received about $1.00 a bushel for his wheat. In 1863, he sold his white wheat for $1.30 a bushel and his red wheat for $1.18. In 1864, the selling price was $2.00 a bushel, and it was $2.50 in 1866. He harvested 564 bushels on his thirty-two acres that year, with an average yield of about 18 bushels per acre. That number was somewhat above the New York State average.[103]

This means there was the wonderful situation in which wheat prices were increasing greatly and farmers were fulfilling a patriotic "duty" to produce as much wheat as they possibly could! It is not surprising at all that farmers would plant wheat on every possible acre of land that could be tilled. This situation—an expanded number of acres planted at a time when wheat prices were more than doubling—clearly led to great profits being made. This was true for Henry K. Dey, so we can begin to assume it was true for other farmers in and around Seneca County. After the Civil War, many farmers built new, grander homes with the profits made from their wartime wheat sales.

The information contained in Henry K. Dey's diaries regarding total wheat production and selling prices for that wheat in the years of the Civil War strongly suggests that the houses along Route 414 were linked to wheat profits during the Civil War years. The most elegant of these "wheat houses" was the one built by Henry Hoster just east of Route 414 on County Road 121. An 1868 Seneca Falls newspaper described Hoster's plans as follows:

> *Mr. Henry Hoster, of Fayette, is building a very fine residence, which, when completed, will be a model of elegance and beauty. It is of the French style of architecture and was designed by Mr. Warren H. Vreeland, an efficient and skillful mechanic of this village. The house will be 42 x 38 feet with a wing 38 x 22 feet, two stories in height and built of brick. The model, plans and drawings of the building are gotten up in a manner rarely excelled and display a degree of taste and appropriateness which places Mr. Vreeland foremost among the best designers and draughtsmen in this section of the State. Mr. Vreeland is doing the carpenter work and there is no doubt that it will be of a superior character. Mr. Hoster has ample means to build*

Built by Henry Hoster, this was the fanciest of the many "wheat houses" between Seneca Falls and Fayette. *Wayne E. Morrison Jr.*

> *with and will spare nothing that is necessary to make his new house in all respects a model structure.*[104]

Miss Buckley said that it cost about $40,000 to build and furnish this house and the surrounding outbuildings. The elegance of this house is suggested in the following words, quoted from the book *Landmarks of Seneca County*: "The 1876 History of Seneca County, New York has a picture of this elegant house in its original state with grounds that included statues placed at intervals about the lawn. The south façade shows beautiful workmanship in the paired, arched windows and their decorative brick trim..."[105] Henry Hoster's new brick house was a major improvement over the much smaller wooden house in which he and his family had been living.

INDUSTRIAL BOOM IN SENECA FALLS AND WATERLOO

The industries in both Seneca Falls and Waterloo secured contracts to supply the Union forces with their war needs. The various pump-making plants in Seneca Falls were providing many of the pumps and other iron products needed in the war efforts. The knitting mills were working at peak capacity. Flour mills expanded their production capacity to keep up with the sharply increasing demand for bread products.

The detailed information about the Seneca Knitting Mills and the Phoenix Woolen Mills in Seneca Falls help us to understand how these industries in both Seneca Falls and Waterloo were shifting to production of war goods. In a late 1861 newspaper article, it was reported:

> *The Seneca Knitting Mills and the Phoenix Woolen Mills, of this village, are both running on Government contracts. The former is making stockings for the Army, and the latter manufacturing blankets for the Navy, and also army cloth. These two Mills are turning out a large amount of work, and give employment to a small army of operatives. The Knitting Mills are now running night and day, and we understand the Phoenix Company will soon be compelled to do the same thing in order to fulfill their contracts.*[106]

In a subsequent article, a Seneca Falls newspaper reported that the Phoenix Mill had received still another contract for the manufacture of navy cloth in the amount of $150,000. That new contract meant that this mill provided over $400,000 worth of goods for the government during the fall and winter months of 1861–62, "aside from the large amount of cloths and cassimeres which they are constantly manufacturing." The plant was then employing over four hundred workers with a monthly payroll of over $15,000.

Similarly, in an 1861 article, a Seneca Falls newspaper reported that the Seneca Knitting Mills had a workforce of between three and four thousand men and women, with many of these workers living in Waterloo and Geneva and over six hundred living in Auburn. The company had ordered more machinery to increase its production capacity by over one-third—turning out about four thousand pairs of hose daily—but still it could not keep up with demand. As a result, orders for many thousands of pairs of stockings had to be turned away. The many female workers at the Seneca Falls mill benefited from good wages that ranged from $0.50 to $1.12. One newspaper article said that the Seneca Knitting Mill had become the largest manufacturing

Many mills in Seneca Falls and Waterloo supplied socks and other clothing items to the military during the Civil War. *Walter Gable.*

company in Seneca Falls—larger even than the pump-making and fire engine companies.[107]

The business boom generated for the war effort generated large profits for Seneca County farmers and industries. Unfortunately, their greatly expanded production levels would set the stage for some serious postwar economic adjustments.

Chapter 11
COPING WITH THE REALITIES OF A PROLONGED WAR

The failure of Union troops to secure victories over Confederate forces in the battles in the first year of the war revealed a harsh reality—a Union victory would be possible only by wearing down the Confederacy in a prolonged war. Democrats, who became known as Copperheads, seized on opportunities to denounce policies of President Lincoln and his Republican cohorts in Congress. With a growing need for more and more troops, Seneca County, like all Northern areas, struggled to meet the increased recruitment quotas.

McClellan Clubs and Politics

As President Lincoln became less and less confident in the ability of General George B. McClellan to head up the Union forces, a McClellan Club was organized in Seneca Falls in early October 1862. Chosen as club president was Josiah T. Miller, a prominent businessman and Democratic Party member. One of the secretaries chosen was Henry Stowell, editor of the *Seneca Falls Reveille*. Resolutions adopted at the organizational meeting included "entire confidence in the statesmanly and soldierly ability, and exalted patriotism of Generals Halleck and McClellan"; that they "regard all attempts of abolition disunionists or others to embarrass the action of the Generals in command, or to undermine their influence and popularity with the army or the people as scarcely less atrocious than the rebellion itself"; and "that a loyal and constitutional opposition party is at all times promotive of the public good; and that such a party was never more required than when the enormous expenditure of public money tends to fill every department of the government with men intent upon speculation and plunder."[108]

The efforts of the McClellan Club probably contributed directly to Horatio Seymour, the Democratic candidate for New York State governor, winning more votes in Seneca County in the 1862 gubernatorial election than did James S. Wadsworth. This result was in contrast to the 1860 gubernatorial election, in which Edwin Morgan, the victorious Republican candidate, had narrowly carried Seneca County, perhaps helped by the favorable results for Abraham Lincoln as the Republican candidate for U.S. president.[109]

As the war dragged on into 1863, there were still more doubts about the actions of Lincoln and his administration. On March 2, 1863, William H. Green of Company C of the Thirty-third New York Volunteers wrote a letter home to his father providing an answer to a question about his feelings about the war:

> *You wish to know how I stand on the war, the Administration, &c. I am in favor of a vigorous prosecution of the war. I am not in favor of peace—that is, I am opposed to all ideas of peace, unless it is a restoration of the Union and a downfall of the so-called Confederacy. I am opposed to all manner of compromises, all foreign intervention, whether by mediation or otherwise. I believe that we are able to settle our own difficulties, and believe that we have some man who is able to command this army. I am no man-lover. I love McClellan as any soldier should his leader, but to go so far as to say that no other than him can command this army, I will not say; but at the same time I cannot see why he is not the man, because he schooled himself for the task, but it seems he did not accomplish anything, after nine months hard drill and school and five months trial. But I am told that he has been meddled with, that his plans have been frustrated by the War Department and the Administration. I say support it to the letter so long as the present one exists, and at another election, if it don't suit, change it. I believe in supporting it, because I believe it to be all powerful. The Union must be preserved at all hazards.*[110]

McClellan Club members saw a real possibility that their support for George B. McClellan might help him win out over Republican Lincoln in the 1864 presidential election. In the 1864 elections, however, Republican incumbent Lincoln carried the popular vote in Seneca County. Democratic incumbent Horatio Seymour was victorious over Republican Reuben Fenton in the gubernatorial election.[111]

QUOTAS AND THE DRAFT IN SENECA COUNTY

Following the initial enlistments in 1861, each state had a quota (based on its proportion of the total population of the Union) of men to enter military service whenever a new call for soldiers was issued by the president. Once the Union instituted a draft, the quota would be filled by conscription (draft) to the extent not offset by volunteers who enlisted. In New York State, each state senatorial district was given a quota proportionate to that district's population as compared with the entire state. Seneca, Ontario and Yates Counties composed the twenty-sixth senatorial district.

As the first draft was being implemented, one Seneca County newspaper editorialized:

> *In common with other localities we shall keenly feel the great sacrifice which the war demands. Few counties in the State have more cheerfully responded to the calls of government than ours, and, few, alas, have realized more fully the terrible effects of this bloody strife. What, then, is the duty of our people in the present emergency? The conscription falls with crushing effect upon the poor man—those who are unable to raise the $300 commutation fee. Shall we see them forced into the service, against every impulse of heart and mind, because of their poverty, or shall we not tax ourselves in each and every town in the county an amount sufficient to pay the commutation of each one drafted? There certainly can be no objection to this measure, and we do not hesitate to urge its adoption. Town meetings can be called in the several towns, the amount voted by the taxable inhabitants, and thus all will share equally the sacrifice which otherwise must fall upon the shoulders of the poor man.*[112]

The editorial went on to point out that Waterloo had already voted to raise by taxation the necessary funds and that other communities within Seneca County were in the process of doing the same.

As the North instituted its first conscription, the new quota for Seneca County was 435. That was soon increased by 50 percent, making for a total of 714 to be conscripted unless there were sufficient volunteers. That was in addition to the number raised in a recent call, forming a total of 769 men to be furnished by Seneca County toward the 600,000 total called for by the U.S. government. Bounties were offered to induce men to volunteer to fill gaps in regiments already in the field. Those enlistments could then be deducted from the county's quota under the new draft law.

Bounties to encourage volunteers had been in existence since the beginning of the war. To help meet the new conscription quotas, the governments of Seneca County and the various towns increased their local bounties. In its December 17, 1863 issue, the *Seneca County Courier* reported that the town of Seneca Falls had upped its bounty to $300 and had agreed to issue $12,000 in town bonds for that purpose "without a dissenting voice" from the more than three hundred citizens who voted on the matter.

A new wave of posters encouraged young men to enlist and get a bigger bounty and avoid the draft. Apparently these increased bounties and recruitment posters were fairly successful. An 1864 newspaper article stated that Seneca County was the first county in the entire state of New York to fill its quota under the last call of the president for 300,000 volunteers. It came, however, with a rather large local government cost. The town of Seneca Falls, for example, incurred an expense of $38,000 to pay the bounties of the last call.

The Seneca County Board of Supervisors was actively involved in 1864 in helping the towns raise their bounty levels, as well as that of the county's own bounty. To begin, on March 24, 1864, the supervisors passed a motion "that some person be appointed to go to the Adjutant General's Office at Albany, to examine the muster rolls of all the Regiments from this State, and ascertain the names of all the men that were credited to the county, and obtain certificates for each town, and forward to the Supervisors of each town in the county." By a follow-up motion, they appointed James M'Lean to be the person to go to Albany. The proceedings do not summarize the discussion surrounding these motions, but they do imply that the county board of supervisors was concerned that "the state" records did not correspond with what local officials felt had been the actual numbers of voluntary enlistments and draftees in each of the towns of Seneca County.

Building on this action, the supervisors on August 5, 1864, passed a motion authorizing the county government to pay to each town a "bounty of Three Hundred Dollars to each Volunteer who shall enlist and be

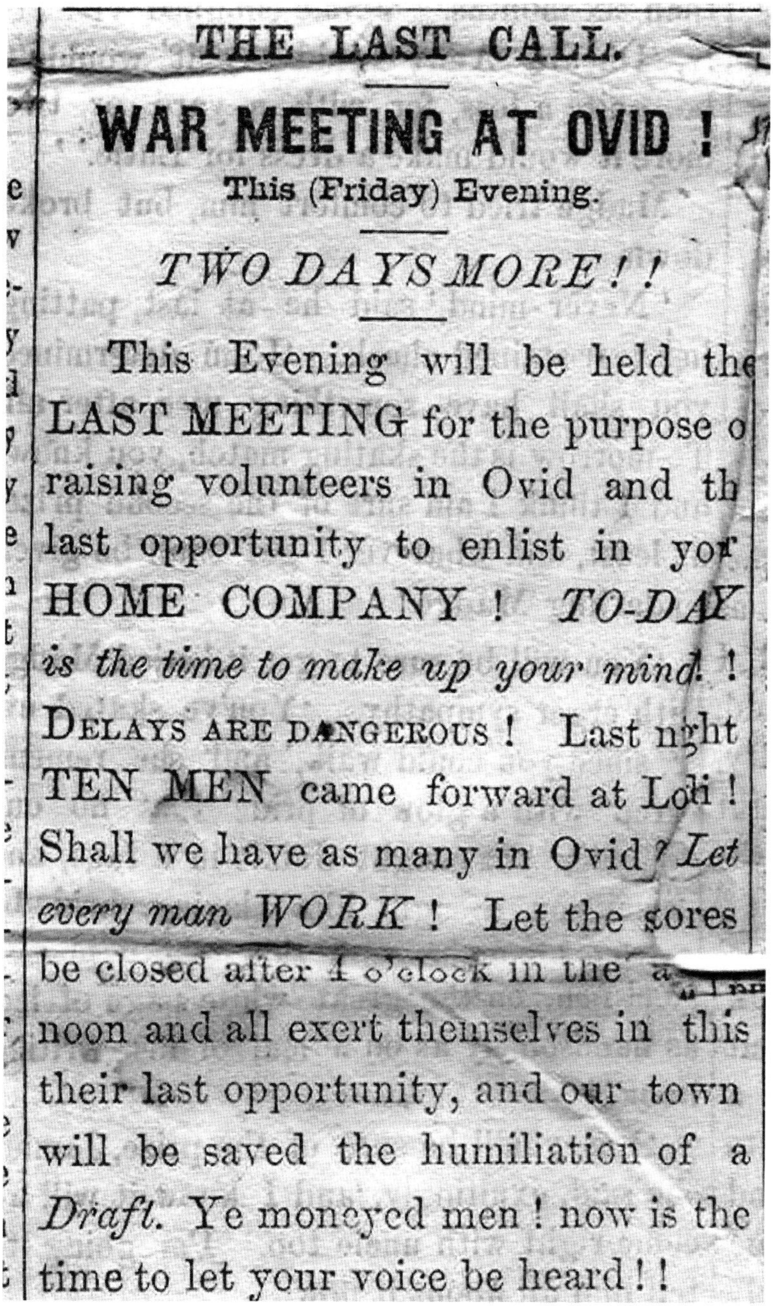

THE LAST CALL.

WAR MEETING AT OVID !

This (Friday) Evening.

TWO DAYS MORE ! !

This Evening will be held the LAST MEETING for the purpose of raising volunteers in Ovid and the last opportunity to enlist in your HOME COMPANY ! *TO-DAY is the time to make up your mind* ! DELAYS ARE DANGEROUS ! Last night TEN MEN came forward at Lodi ! Shall we have as many in Ovid ? *Let every man WORK* ! Let the stores be closed after 4 o'clock in the afternoon and all exert themselves in this their last opportunity, and our town will be saved the humiliation of a *Draft*. Ye moneyed men ! now is the time to let your voice be heard ! !

The new conscription law prompted local meetings to discuss how best to meet the need for more soldiers. *Roberta Halden.*

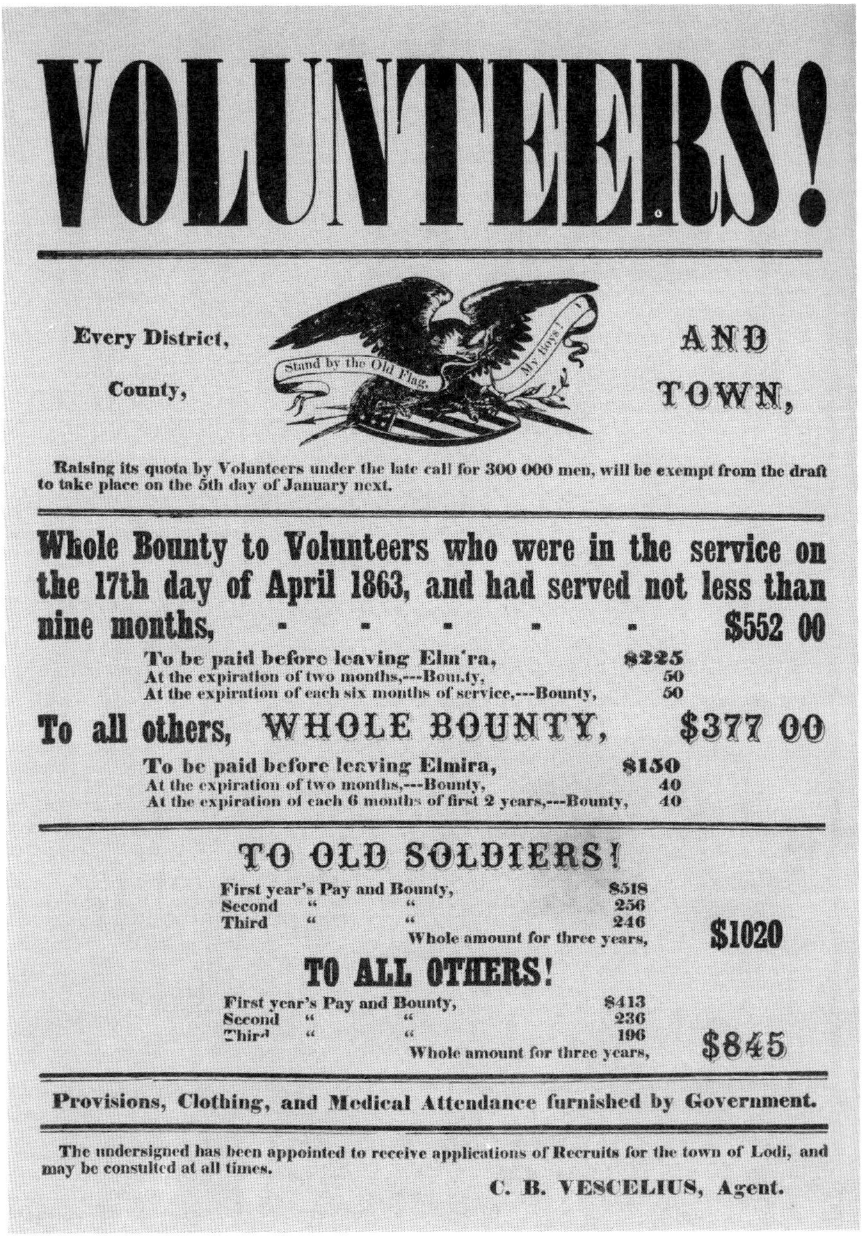

VOLUNTEERS!

Every District, County, AND TOWN,

Stand by the Old Flag, My Boys!

Raising its quota by Volunteers under the late call for 300 000 men, will be exempt from the draft to take place on the 5th day of January next.

Whole Bounty to Volunteers who were in the service on the 17th day of April 1863, and had served not less than nine months, - - - - - $552 00

To be paid before leaving Elm'ra,	$225
At the expiration of two months,---Bounty,	50
At the expiration of each six months of service,---Bounty,	50

To all others, WHOLE BOUNTY, $377 00

To be paid before leaving Elmira,	$150
At the expiration of two months,---Bounty,	40
At the expiration of each 6 months of first 2 years,---Bounty,	40

TO OLD SOLDIERS!

First year's Pay and Bounty,		$518	
Second "	"	256	
Third "	"	246	
	Whole amount for three years,		$1020

TO ALL OTHERS!

First year's Pay and Bounty,		$413	
Second "	"	236	
Third "	"	196	
	Whole amount for three years,		$845

Provisions, Clothing, and Medical Attendance furnished by Government.

The undersigned has been appointed to receive applications of Recruits for the town of Lodi, and may be consulted at all times.

C. B. VESCELIUS, Agent.

Above: An April 1863 recruitment poster in Ovid showing an increased bounty for enlistees. *Wayne E. Morrison Jr.*

Opposite: Quotas for each of the Seneca County towns as of July 2, 1862. From the *Seneca County Courier*.

Co. M---Capt. Bennett Munger, Penn Yan.
1st Lieut. Elzor B. James, Italy.
2d " Charles Kelly, Penn Yan.

Quota for Seneca County,

The following statement shows the quota of each town in this county towards the 600,000 volunteers called for since July 2, 1862:

TOWNS.	Quota.	Furn-ished.	Surp's	Deficit
Covert,	74	78	4	
Fayette,	115	130	15	
Junius,	44	25		19
Lodi'	64	66	2	
Ovid,	78	86	8	
Romulus,	67	70	3	
Seneca Falls,	184	186	2	
Tyre,	44	45	1	
Varick,	58	64	6	
Waterloo,	142	159	17	
Total,	870	909	39	

mustered into the United States service under the late call of the President for 500,000 men, dated July 18, 1864, until the quota of the County is filled under said call, or the Draft takes place." That same motion authorized the county to pay a person fifteen dollars for each enlisted volunteer he or she secured. Interestingly, the motion also authorized one or more county agents to obtain recruits from the "Rebel States, such recruits to receive two hundred and fifty dollars, and to be credited to the quota of said county, and distributed to the several towns in proportion to the quota of said town under the present call." These recruits from the Southern states would help fill Seneca County's quota. Seneca County was simply implementing a proposal that had come from the adjutant general's office. The Seneca County Board of Supervisors voted to issue bonds to pay for the expenses of all of these recruitment and enlistment bounties. Clearly the county board was authorizing expenditures of county funds to help secure the additional troops needed for the Union to win the war.

Apparently a county bounty of $300 was not sufficient to fill the quota of the towns of Seneca County. The county bounty for each enlistment was raised to $800 at the board's special meeting on August 25, 1864. The minutes for that meeting also stated that William H. Burton was the county's agent in the Rebel states to procure recruits for this county's quota.

At the board's annual meeting on November 24, 1864, Fayette supervisor William M. Stacey offered a "request to the Governor of the State of New York, in relation to the unjust enlistment and drafting of men into the U.S. service." The matter was tabled. There is no further information to help explain what prompted this action.[113]

From the minutes of the board's December 2, 1864 meeting, however, we get a sense of what "unjust enlistment and drafting of men" was all about. At that meeting, the board voted to send a letter to the New York State Assembly and Senate urging that existing state laws be changed so that men who enlist in a community outside of their county or town of known residence would be counted toward the quota for their town of residence. For example, the Seneca County Board of Supervisors was concerned that Seneca County residents who enlisted in either Auburn or Geneva were being counted toward the quota for Cayuga County (in the case of enlistments in Auburn) or Ontario County (in the case of enlistments in Geneva).[114]

Despite all these bounties, at least 444 Seneca County men were drafted into military service.

Part III

LEST WE FORGET: PRESERVING THE LEGACY

We here highly resolve that these dead shall not have died in vain…
—President Abraham Lincoln, Gettysburg Address, November 19, 1863

Chapter 12

WATERLOO: BIRTHPLACE OF MEMORIAL DAY

Memorial Day is an official day of remembrance for those who have died in our nation's service during wartime. For many Americans, however, Memorial Day weekend marks an unofficial beginning to the joys of summer. That is not so in the Seneca County community of Waterloo, which has been officially recognized as the birthplace of Memorial Day. Each year on May 30, regardless of which day of the week that date occurs, Waterloo residents gather for a parade and solemn cemetery event.

A Short History of Memorial Day

Memorial Day was officially proclaimed by General John A. Logan, the national commander of the Grand Army of the Republic (GAR), in his General Order No. 11 on May 5, 1868. In this order, Logan gave instructions for all GAR posts throughout the country on May 30, 1868 (and every year thereafter on that date), to strew with flowers or otherwise decorate "the graves of comrades who died in defense of their country during the late rebellion." Logan did not prescribe any specific form of ceremony, but the order stated that "posts and comrades will in their own way arrange such fitting services and testimonials of respect as circumstances may permit."[115] Following is the full text of General Order No. 11:

> *The 30th day of May 1868 is designated for the purpose of strewing with flowers or otherwise decorating the graves of comrades who died in defense of their country during the late rebellion, and whose bodies now lie in almost every city, village, and hamlet church-yard in the land. In this observance no form of ceremony is prescribed, but posts and comrades will in their own way arrange such fitting services and testimonials of respect as circumstances may permit.*
>
> *We are organized, comrades, as our regulations tell us, for the purpose among other things, "of preserving and strengthening those kind and fraternal feelings which have bound together the soldiers, sailors, and marines who united to suppress the late rebellion." What can aid more to assure this result than cherishing tenderly the memory of our heroic dead, who made their breasts a barricade between our country and its foes? Their soldier lives were the reveille of freedom to a race in chains, and their deaths the tattoo of rebellious tyranny in arms. We should guard their graves with sacred vigilance. All that the consecrated wealth and taste of the nation can add to their adornment and security is but a fitting tribute to the memory of her slain defenders. Let no wanton foot tread rudely on such hallowed grounds. Let pleasant paths invite the coming and going of reverent visitors and fond mourners. Let no vandalism of avarice or neglect, no ravages of time testify to the present or to the coming generations that we have forgotten as a people the cost of a free and undivided republic.*
>
> *If other eyes grow dull, other hands slack, and other hearts cold in the solemn trust, ours shall keep it well as long as the light and warmth of life remain to us.*
>
> *Let us, then, at the time appointed gather around their sacred remains and garland the passionless mounds above them with the choicest flowers of spring-time; let us raise above them the dear old flag they saved from dishonor; let us in this solemn presence renew our pledges to aid and assist those whom they have left among us a sacred charge upon a nation's gratitude, the soldier's and sailor's widow and orphan.*
>
> *It is the purpose of the Commander-in-Chief to inaugurate this observance with the hope that it will be kept up from year to year, while a survivor of the war remains to honor the memory of his departed comrades.*

He earnestly desires the public press to lend its friendly aid in bringing to the notice of comrades in all parts of the country in time for simultaneous compliance therewith.

Department commanders will use efforts to make this order effective.

By order of
JOHN A. LOGAN, Commander-in-Chief
N.P. CHIPMAN, Adjutant General
Official: WM. T. COLLINS, A.A.G.[116]

Implementing Logan's General Order No. 11, communities throughout the northern states held an observance on May 30, 1868. This practice continued annually and became known as Decoration Day, largely because a common event was decorating the graves of the fallen Union soldiers with spring flowers.

The first large observance (an estimated five thousand people attended) at Arlington National Cemetery, across the Potomac River from Washington, D.C., was held in 1868. The ceremonies centered on the mourning-draped veranda of the Arlington mansion that had been the home of General Robert E. Lee. Various Washington officials, including General and Mrs. Ulysses S. Grant, presided over the ceremonies. After speeches, children from the Soldiers' and Sailors' Orphan Home and members of the GAR made their way through the cemetery, placing flowers on both Union and Confederate graves, reciting prayers and singing hymns. Since the late 1950s, as part of the annual Memorial Day observances at Arlington National Cemetery, a small American flag is placed on each grave, making for a most moving sight.[117]

On May 30, 1870, General Logan gave an address in honor of this new commemorative holiday. In that address, he said:

This Memorial Day, on which we decorate their graves with the tokens of love and affection, is no idle ceremony with us, to pass away an hour; but it brings back to our minds in all their vividness the fearful conflicts of that terrible war in which they fell as victims…Let us, then, all unite in the solemn feelings of the hour, and tender with our flowers the warmest sympathies of our souls! Let us revive our patriotism and love of country by this act, and strengthen our loyalty by the example of the noble dead around us.[118]

The first state to officially recognize the holiday as a state holiday was New York in 1873. By 1890, it was recognized by all the northern states. Southern states refused to acknowledge the day, honoring their dead on a different day until after World War I.[119]

The preferred name for the holiday gradually changed from Decoration Day to Memorial Day after World War II. The official name of Memorial Day was proclaimed by federal law in 1967. On June 28, 1968, the Uniform Monday Holiday Act passed by Congress moved Memorial Day to the last Monday in May so as to create a three-day weekend. As a result, starting in May 1971, Memorial Day was not always on May 30. Within a few years, all fifty states adopted Congress's change in date. Several southern states have an additional day for honoring their Confederate war dead: January 19 in Texas; April 26 in Alabama, Florida, Georgia and Mississippi; May 10 in South Carolina; and June 3 in Louisiana and Tennessee.

In 1915, Moina Michael began the practice of wearing red poppies on Memorial Day to honor those who died serving the nation during war. Shortly before Memorial Day in 1922, the Veterans of Foreign Wars became the first veterans' organization to sell poppies nationally. Two years later, their Buddy Poppy Program was selling artificial poppies made by disabled veterans. In 1948, the U.S. Post Office honored Ms. Michael for her role in founding the national poppy movement by issuing a three-cent stamp with her likeness on it.

To help reeducate and remind Americans of the true meaning of Memorial Day, Congress passed the National Moment of Remembrance Resolution in December 2000. It asks that at 3:00 p.m. local time, all Americans "voluntarily and informally observe in their own way a Moment of remembrance and respect, pausing from whatever they are doing for a moment of silence or listening to 'Taps.'"[120]

EVENTS IN WATERLOO

The story of the birth of Memorial Day in Waterloo begins in the summer of 1865 with a prominent local druggist, Henry C. Welles. Welles mentioned to some of his friends at a social gathering that while praising the living veterans of the Civil War, it would be well to remember the patriotic dead

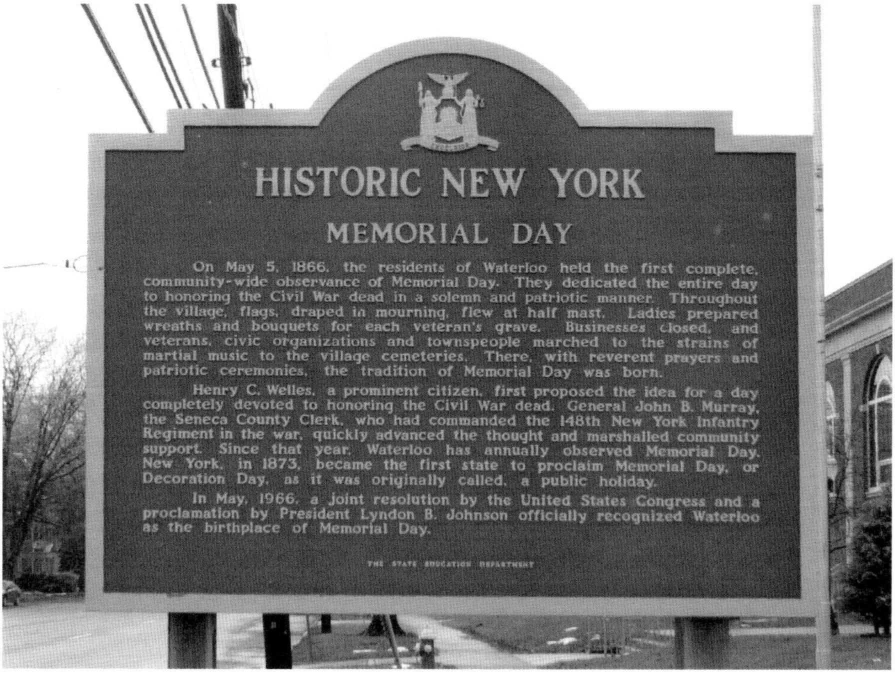

The New York State Historic Area marker in Lafayette Park describing the events in Waterloo that led to the community being recognized as the birthplace of Memorial Day. *Walter Gable.*

by placing flowers on their graves. Nothing resulted from this suggestion until he advanced the idea again the following spring to Brigadier General John B. Murray, an intensely patriotic Civil War hero and at the time the Seneca County clerk. Brigadier General Murray supported the idea wholeheartedly and marshaled veterans' support. Plans were developed for a more complete celebration by a local citizens' committee headed by Welles and Murray.

On May 5, 1866, all businesses were closed, and the village was decorated with flags at half-mast, draped with evergreens and mourning black. The women of the village gathered at Towsley Hall on Virginia Street to make bouquets of lilacs and pine branches. Veterans, civil societies and residents, led by General Murray, marched to the strains of martial music to the three village cemeteries. There, impressive ceremonies were held, including placing bouquets on each of the graves of fallen comrades, as well as offering prayers and speeches commemorating their sacrifice for their country.[121] The ceremonies at each cemetery were "somewhat long" and the day

Henry C. Welles was the Waterloo druggist who first suggested an organized event in Waterloo to honor Union dead from the Civil War. *Waterloo Historical Society*.

oppressively hot, with the result that "several persons were exhausted before the ceremonies were closed." Henry C. Welles was among those people, and it is said that he never recovered from the effects.

Author John E. Becker, in his *A History of the Village of Waterloo*, noted, "In a sense it was a daring gesture. There were men on that beautiful May morning who were not sure just how the rank and file of the soldiers would take it. Dissention was in their ranks, but they did not falter, and every

John B. Murray worked with Henry C. Welles in developing the plans for May 5, 1866 events in Waterloo to honor the Union dead in the Civil War. *Waterloo Historical Society*.

soldier, sailor and marine, whose body lay in the cemeteries, had flowers placed upon his grave. Thus ended the day that was to be hailed across the country as the beginning of Decoration Day."[122]

One year later, on May 5, 1867, the ceremonies were repeated. During 1867, General Murray discussed Waterloo's commemoration with General John A. Logan, commander of the GAR. General Logan felt that all GAR posts should observe this commemoration. To implement this action, he

East Main Street, Waterloo, 1866. *Waterloo Historical Society.*

issued his General Order No. 11 directing that Memorial Day be observed on May 30, 1868, and every year thereafter. In 1868, Waterloo joined with other communities in holding their observance on May 30, in accordance with General Logan's orders.

Waterloo residents commonly refer to General John B. Murray as the "Father of Decoration Day." This is largely because of his military service during the Civil War; the speech he gave as part of the May 5, 1867 ceremonies; and the fact that he "influenced" General Logan to issue his General Order No. 11. The important role played by Henry C. Welles should not, however, be overlooked. In a speech given by Reverend William S. Carter, pastor of the Waterloo Presbyterian Church, to the members of the Waterloo GAR post at the Memorial Day Service in 1886, Reverend Carter said, "The idea itself [for Decoration Day] really found its incipiency in the brain of Henry C. Welles, whom you remember as a citizen of this place."[123]

DOCUMENTING THE WATERLOO EVENTS

The events of the Memorial Day observances in Waterloo were printed in the *Waterloo Observer*, but all copies of the paper were destroyed in the newspaper office fire of 1877. Fortunately, there is other extensive documentary evidence of the Waterloo events.

Word spread throughout the nation of Waterloo as the original place at which Decoration Day was observed. The Waterloo events were mentioned in national and state encampments of the GAR. The editor of the *Neighbor's Home Mail*, a widely read magazine published in Phelps, New York, gave to each of its subscribers a fine life-sized portrait, suitable for framing, of General John B. Murray with the inscription "Father of Decoration Day."

The *Colorado Catholic* contained an article that noted, "The first public demonstration in decorating the graves of federal soldiers in the North took place at Waterloo, New York, the place where Reverend L.A. Lambert, the efficient Chaplain of the Eighteenth Illinois Volunteers, delivered the excellent memorial address, printed on the first page of this paper. The National holiday known as Decoration Day had its beginning from this demonstration. We remember the occasion well."

An article published in *The Banner*, the official publication of the Sons of Union Veterans of the Civil War, said the following about the origin of Memorial Day:

> *The morning of May 5, 1866, dawned clear and beautiful in the little town of Waterloo, New York. It was a morning that was to see the beginning of a beautiful, sacred and solemn custom, a practice that was eventually to become accepted and universally practiced by the American people. On that pleasant morning, General John B. Murray, then a resident of Waterloo, conceived the idea of calling together a platoon of ex-soldiers who had worn the Blue of the Northland during the War of the Rebellion, for the purpose of showing by their action, their intense loyalty, their love and devotion toward those of their comrades who had answered the last roll call.*
>
> *Visualize to yourself what a scene this must have been. Flags floating proudly on the balmy spring breeze; flowers piled in great profusion; flowers that had been gathered by the school children previous to this occasion; members of that large body of soldiers who comprised the Union Army during the War that, only a year previous, they had brought to a successful conclusion.*
>
> *Standing at attention these soldiers received perhaps from the hands of the school children these first blossoms of spring. Those men were in the prime of their life, and with heads erect, shoulders thrown back, at the command of*

General Murray, marched to the strains of martial music to the local cemetery and proceeded to decorate the graves of their departed comrades.

That morning, beautiful with the first blossoms of spring; the birds gaily singing; the air sweet with the perfume of flowers; the trees resplendent in their green foliage; all nature seemed to be fitted for this sacred duty. Even the Ruler of the Universe seemed in accord with these Men in Blue; this God of Love and Mercy who had carried them safely through the strife and turmoil of war, seemed to smile benignly down upon these Men in Blue, who with reverential respect, with heads bowed with love and devotion, made this first public showing of their love and devotion for their departed comrades.[124]

OFFICIAL RECOGNITION OF WATERLOO

Waterloo has been officially recognized for holding the first formal, village-wide, annual observance of a day dedicated to honoring the war dead.

Lafayette Park monument using the Waterloo-Birthplace of Memorial Day logo. *Walter Gable.*

State of New York

Executive Chamber

On May 5, 1866, the citizens of Waterloo, with stores closed, flags flying at half-mast draped in mourning, with wreath and cross and martial music, marched to the village cemeteries to eulogize the fallen heroes of the Civil War and lay floral offerings on their graves. This was the first formal, complete, well-planned, village-wide observance of a day entirely dedicated to honoring the war dead. The observance was held two years before General John A. Logan issued his famous order Number 11 formally proclaiming Memorial (Decoration) Day.

These facts are corroborated by documents from authentic sources. The people of Waterloo are justly proud of this outstanding event in the history of their community. They are planning a solemn and colorful celebration of the 100th anniversary of the first Memorial Day observance held in their village. It is fitting that the rest of us, their fellow citizens of the Empire State, participate in this celebration.

SO, THEREFORE, I, Nelson A. Rockefeller, Governor of the State of New York, do hereby proclaim Waterloo, New York as the

BIRTHPLACE OF MEMORIAL DAY

to be so honored throughout the State of New York.

G I V E N under my hand and the Privy Seal of the State at the Capitol in the City of Albany this seventh day of March in the year of our Lord one thousand nine hundred and sixty-six.

BY THE GOVERNOR

Governor Rockefeller's proclamation recognizing Waterloo as the birthplace of Memorial Day. *Waterloo Historical Society*.

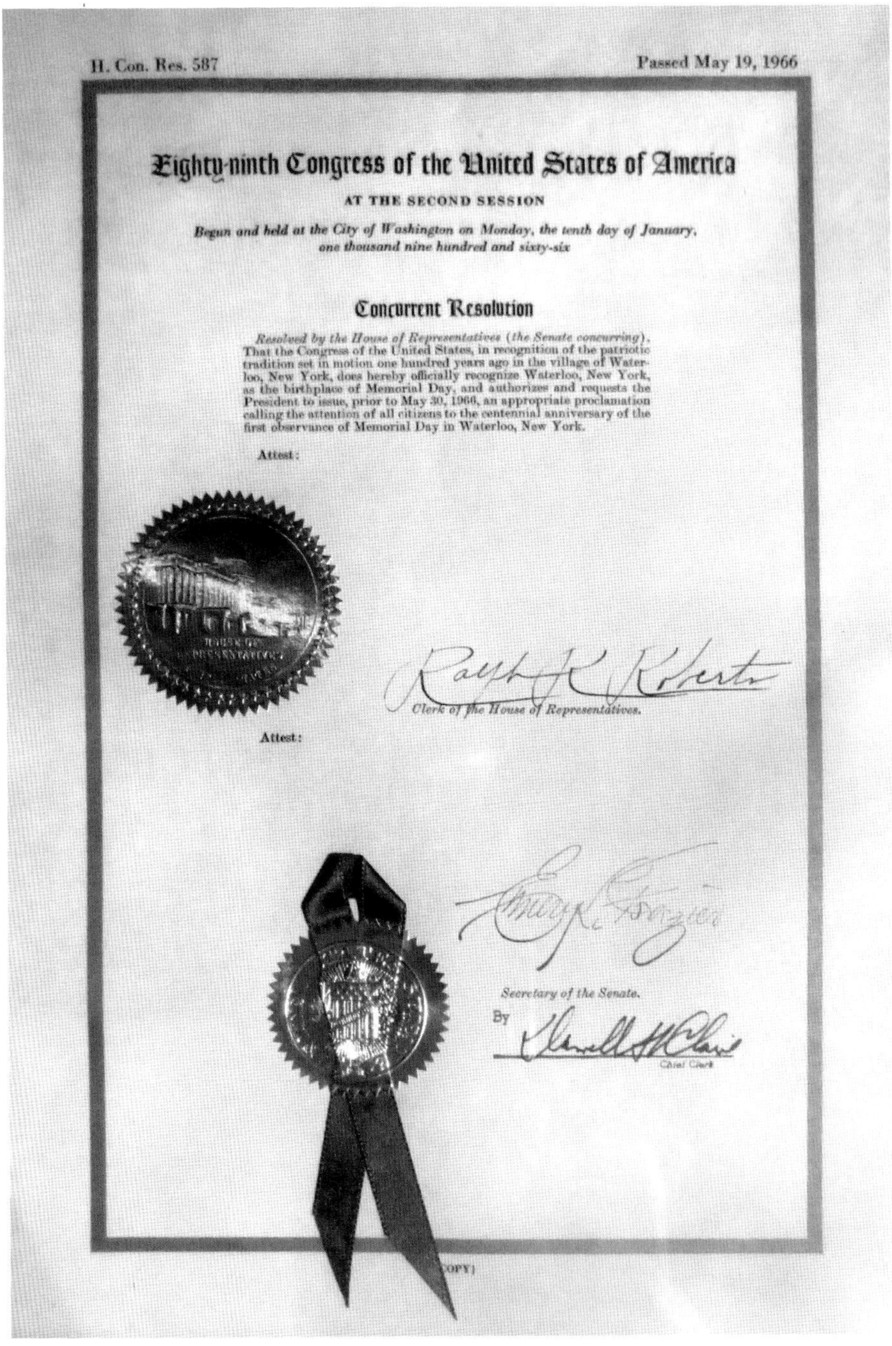

H. Con. Res. 587 Passed May 19, 1966

Eighty-ninth Congress of the United States of America

AT THE SECOND SESSION

Begun and held at the City of Washington on Monday, the tenth day of January, one thousand nine hundred and sixty-six

Concurrent Resolution

Resolved by the House of Representatives (the Senate concurring), That the Congress of the United States, in recognition of the patriotic tradition set in motion one hundred years ago in the village of Waterloo, New York, does hereby officially recognize Waterloo, New York, as the birthplace of Memorial Day, and authorizes and requests the President to issue, prior to May 30, 1966, an appropriate proclamation calling the attention of all citizens to the centennial anniversary of the first observance of Memorial Day in Waterloo, New York.

Attest:

Clerk of the House of Representatives.

Attest:

Secretary of the Senate.

By

Chief Clerk

Congressional resolution recognizing Waterloo as the birthplace of Memorial Day. *Waterloo Historical Society*.

After signing his proclamation recognizing Waterloo as the birthplace of Memorial Day, President Lyndon B. Johnson shook hands with Congressman Sam Stratton, whose district included Waterloo. *Waterloo Historical Society*.

On March 7, 1966, the State of New York recognized Waterloo in the form of a proclamation signed by Governor Nelson A. Rockefeller. This was followed by recognition from the U.S. Congress and the passing of Concurrent Resolution 587 (which was passed May 17 in the House of Representatives and May 19 in the Senate). The resolution read, in part: "Resolved that the Congress of the United States, in recognition of the patriotic tradition set in motion one hundred years ago in the Village of Waterloo, New York, does hereby officially recognize Waterloo, New York, as the birthplace of Memorial Day." On May 26, 1966, President Lyndon B. Johnson signed a presidential proclamation (which is on display at the National Memorial Day Museum) recognizing Waterloo as the birthplace of Memorial Day. It was in 1967 that President Johnson signed legislation officially changing the name of the holiday from Decoration Day to Memorial Day.[125]

OTHER PLACES CLAIM TO BE THE BIRTHPLACE OF MEMORIAL DAY

Even though Waterloo has been officially recognized as the birthplace of Memorial Day, there are other communities that have made that claim. According to the U.S. Department of Veterans Affairs, roughly two dozen places claim to be the primary source of the holiday. This assertion is based on information found on plaques and websites and/or in claims of local historians. It seems that each of these rival claims uses different criteria—whether its ceremony was, in fact, the earliest to honor the Civil War dead, the first one that General Logan heard about or the first one that conceived of a national, recurring day of commemoration and honor.[126]

One such claim originates in Boalsburg, Pennsylvania. In the summer and fall of 1864, women put flowers on the graves of their own Civil War dead from the battle at nearby Gettysburg and on other Civil War dead. In August 1868, the Boalsburg chapter of the GAR took on the responsibility of a yearly observance.

In April 1865, some women in Vicksburg, Mississippi, went to the cemetery to decorate the graves of soldiers. This action was led by Mrs. Sue Landon Vaught, a descendant of President John Adams.

In May 1865, local women in Winchester, Virginia, formed the Stonewall Jackson Memorial Association and decorated all the graves in the Confederate Cemetery. This was supposedly the first cemetery established for dead soldiers in the South.[127]

On April 25, 1866, women in Columbus, Mississippi, went to "Friendship" Cemetery, the burial ground for the Shiloh battle dead, and laid flowers on both Union and Confederate graves. Horace Greeley's *New York Tribune* printed a story on the unprejudiced acts of these women that led to widespread interest in impartial offerings to the memory of the Civil War dead. Their action was described as a "healing touch for the nation."[128]

Still another place that claimed to be the birthplace of Memorial Day was Carbondale, Illinois. In April 1866, Ambrose Crowell, Russell Winchester and Jonathan F. Wiseman were inspired by seeing a woman with two children putting flowers on the graves in the rural Hiller Cemetery just outside the city. The three men cleaned and decorated other graves that day. They then organized a wide-scale memorial observance at the larger Carbondale Woodlawn Cemetery on April 29. As part of that observance, 219 Civil War veterans marched to the cemetery. Major General John A. Logan, a resident of southern Illinois, gave the principal speech.[129]

In his book *Race and Reunion: The Civil War in American Memory*, David W. Blight, a professor of history at Yale University, described an almost forgotten event in Charleston, South Carolina, that occurred in 1865. At a racetrack turned into a war prison, black workmen properly reburied the Union dead who were found there. On May 1, 1865, a cemetery dedication was held, with thousands of freed blacks marching in procession around the track. Blight suggested that this might be the first Memorial Day, as it predated most of the other contenders. His argument is weakened by the fact that he could find no evidence that it led to General Logan's call for a national holiday.[130]

The arguments of these communities, as well as others not mentioned above, might sound meritorious. The bottom line to all of these claims, however, is that Waterloo has been recognized by both presidential proclamation and congressional resolution as the official birthplace of Memorial Day. Probably the most compelling factor is that the events in Waterloo can be directly linked to General Logan issuing his General Order No. 11, which called for an annual commemoration each May 30 on the part of local GAR chapters throughout the country.

THE NATIONAL MEMORIAL DAY MUSEUM

The National Memorial Day Museum is located at 35 East Main Street in Waterloo. The front parlor of this former private residence is decorated as if the family residents are in mourning for the loss of a family member in a Civil War battle. The two other parlors and dining room

The National Memorial Day Museum in Waterloo has many displays and extensive archives. *Walter Gable.*

have interpretative exhibits about Waterloo events in 1866 that became the origins of Memorial Day, as well as artifacts and documents of various soldiers and military units. The second floor includes other exhibits, as well as extensive document storage and a research room.[131]

The Annual Celebrate Commemorate Festivities in Waterloo

Starting in 2000, the Waterloo community has held a series of events known as Celebrate Commemorate during Memorial Day weekend. The weekend begins on Friday night with a solemn Illumination Ceremony at the American Civil War Memorial. In recognition of its healing role, Waterloo's Illumination Ceremony includes a benediction and invocation from Union

Female reenactors on Oak Island during the 2013 Celebrate/Commemorate Weekend. *Walter Gable.*

and Confederate chaplains and the participation of reenactor units from both sides. There is also a reading of the names of the 58 Waterloo Fallen, followed by the placing of luminaries on each of their markers.[132]

On Saturday and Sunday, there is a series of Civil War living history events at Oak Island, including encampments by Civil War reenactors, boat trips on the Cayuga-Seneca Canal, musical entertainment and programs and fireworks on Saturday night. In Lafayette Park, there are exhibits by vendors, food and beverage sales, wagon tours of the village and musical entertainment on the stage. On Saturday morning, there is a big parade. On Sunday, there is a car show, including Woodie vehicles made in Waterloo. Throughout the village, there are other programs and events at various places, including the National Memorial Day Museum, the M'Clintock House of the Women's Rights National Historical Park and the Waterloo Library and Historical Society.

The actual official celebration/commemoration of Memorial Day, however, still takes place on May 30 each year, regardless of which day of the week that date falls on. The day is marked with a big parade and a cemetery ceremony that includes a reciting of General Logan's General Order No. 11.

Chapter 13

THE SCYTHE TREE STORY

Many cities and villages in New York State have a Civil War monument. They serve as silent markers of "the life blood spilt, that a country might live and that a race be freed."[133] One of the most unusual Civil War monuments is the Scythe Tree. This is not a monument

Postcard of the Scythe Tree showing two of the scythe blades. *Waterloo Historical Society*.

The Scythe Tree as it looked in 2011. *Walter Gable.*

of brass or marble but one of living wood.[134] The Scythe Tree is a living monument to young men going off to war. The Scythe Tree is located at 841 Waterloo-Geneva Road, two miles west of Waterloo on Routes 5 and 20. The tree itself is a balm of Gilead, a variety of poplar rarely found in this part of the state.

The following poem about the Scythe Tree was written by Clinton Scollard in 1911:

The Scythe Tree

Farmer Johnson strode from the field
With an eager step that was long and lithe;
The summer sun, like a blazing shield,
Burned on high in the hazy sky.
A forked bough, as he hastened by,
Seemed a fitting place for his scythe;
So he swung it up in the balsam tree;
"There let it hang till I come," said he.

Then he homeward hied him, humming a tune,
But he heard a word at the farmstead gate
Under the fervid heat of the noon,
A ringing call to each volunteer,
For all the land was alive with fear,
Doubt and fear for the country's fate.
So farmer Johnson shouldered his gun
And left his scythe to the rain and sun.

Fifty years have sped since then;
Fifty hastening years and more;
By Southern wood and brake and fen
Faithful he fought, and in gallant wise,
Fought and died, and now he lies
By the far off Carolina shore,
Where the long trades blow and the grasses wave
Over the loam of his sunken grave.

"There let it hang till I come," he said,
Of the scythe he left in the balsam tree;
And they let it hang, as the fleet days fled,
Till the small hole, fed by the kindly earth,
Clasped the scythe with a mothering girth.
Today whoever so will may see
The starry emblem of freedom flow
Over the tip of the scythe below.

He gave his all, and he never came;
He that was strong and young and lithe,
But the balsam boughs seem to name his name;
Name his name both late and long
To the tuneful beat of a summer song,
To the undulant sway-song of the scythe;
And the banner swings to the rhythmic bars,
The banner he loved, the Stripes and Stars.

Enlistment of James Wyman Johnson

Following the fall of Fort Sumter in April 1861, the nation was swept with war fever. President Abraham Lincoln called for troops, and thousands of brave men and boys rushed to arms. Recruiting officers visited this section of the country and held patriotic meetings in the district schoolhouses and churches to get recruits for the Union army. One evening in the early fall of 1861, James Wyman Johnson attended one of these meetings, held in the Vail District schoolhouse. He was the eldest son of James and Elizabeth Goodhue Johnson. Altogether, two daughters and two sons lived with their parents on the family's small farm. James had been born at Pennfield, New Hampshire, on January 1, 1835. At this fall 1861 recruiting meeting at the Vail District schoolhouse, "many hard-handed farmers and their sons gathered that night and listened with mixed emotions and drawn faces to the appeal of the recruiting agents; it must have been much like an old fashioned revival."[135] Johnson was particularly impressed by the arguments of the Reverend Samuel H. Gridley, pastor of the First Presbyterian Church of Waterloo. His comments made Johnson feel as if it were his duty to respond and, if need be, give his life for his country. He was torn, however, by his responsibilities to his family and the farm. Which was more important—his patriotic duty or his duty to family and the farm?

Still pondering this question the following morning, Johnson went out into the field to mow. While swinging the scythe, he decided he needed to enlist. Hastening to the house, he told his parents of his intention. He carefully placed the scythe in the crotch of the tree and allegedly said, "Leave this scythe in the tree until I return." It needs to be noted that

Drawing of the Johnson Farm with the scythe tree as it probably looked in 1861. *Waterloo Historical Society.*

at that time, the tree was a young sapling about eight inches in diameter and just a few feet in height. Fighting back the tears streaming down their cheeks, his parents consented to his wishes, and young Johnson prepared to enlist. On October 29, 1861, he enlisted in Company G of the Eighty-fifth New York Volunteers, commanded by Captain John Raines of Canandaigua and composed of several young men from Seneca County.[136] At the time of his enlistment, he was twenty-six years old and was described as a serious, slim, beardless, blue-eyed young man of medium height (believed to be five feet, ten inches tall) with dark hair neatly combed.[137]

James Wyman Johnson in his military uniform. *Waterloo Historical Society*.

The Evils of His Military Service

After many months of hardship and fighting, Wyman Johnson (he is known as Wyman in the military records) returned home in 1863 for furlough. His parents were shaken by his bearded, melancholy face, which made him look twice his age and visibly demonstrated the harsh realities of the war experiences. At the end of his furlough, he returned to battle, leaving behind his heartbroken parents and the scythe—still hanging in the tree.[138]

Wyman's military experiences continued to be unpleasant. He was taken prisoner in New Berne, North Carolina, and held in one of the war prisons. He was later released, probably in an exchange of prisoners, and went back into battle still again. On April 20, 1864, the now Sergeant Wyman Johnson was wounded in the upper thigh at Plymouth, North Carolina, by a blast from a small carbine. Realizing that he was likely to die, he gave his reenlistment money to his friend Lieutenant Edwin Pierson and asked him to give the money to his parents. (Edwin was very soon forced to march to Andersonville prison, and we do not know what happened to Johnson's money). As one of the wounded, Wyman was treated by overworked Confederate surgeons until about mid-May, at which point he and the other wounded were moved out to make room for more Confederate troops. He was then taken with the severely wounded soldiers to the Confederate Hospital at Raleigh, North Carolina.[139] He died there on May 22, 1864, from his wounds and was buried in an unknown grave.[140]

Family Tried to Learn of His Whereabouts

News of the whereabouts of Wyman Johnson was slow getting back to his family in Waterloo. The scythe remained in the poplar tree near the kitchen door, a constant reminder of the elder son's absence. Rumors spread about the fate of the "Plymouth Pilgrims"—many of those soldiers captured at the Plymouth, North Carolina battle and now being held at Andersonville Prison, where a third of the company would die of typhoid, dysentery, smallpox or starvation. In December 1864, Wyman's sister Julia Ann wrote to the surgeon general. Surgeon William T. Comstock wrote back on January 16, 1865, saying that Wyman had

> *received a severe wound of the middle 3rd of the right thigh, the ball lodging near the bone and fracturing the same. We remained at Plymouth til May 15th when we removed to Raleigh, N.C. The journey was a very severe one, which so exhausted him that at 6 o'clock of the morning of the 22nd of May, he breathed his last. He was conscious until within a few minutes of his death. I dressed his wound from the day he received his injury to the day of his death. I never once heard him complain. He was conscious of his danger, and wished me to inform his friends of his fate. This was the only request he made. As he never seemed willing to converse during his sickness, I did not exact anything further from him...The rebel surgeons, I must say, were very kind, and did all they could. The medicines, dressing and diet were good.*[141]

On hearing the news of the death of their son, the parents refused to believe it. They prayed that he would someday return to them. They kept their faith that he would return until their death—the father died nine years after his son and the mother a year later.[142]

The family home was left in the care of Wyman's sister Julia Ann Johnson, who had suffered another sorrow in that her fiancé, Tyler J. Snyder, had been killed in action at Gettysburg on July 2, 1863. Miss Julia Ann Johnson considered it almost a vow to keep the scythe of her brother in the crotch of the tree where he had hung it. Years passed, and the handle fell away. The tree grew and gradually surrounded the blade. The long scythe blade protruded only a few inches outside the mammoth tree trunk. An American flag was kept on the tree for many years by Miss Johnson. She also draped black crepe on the tip of the scythe blade.[143]

It was not until 1916 that the actual burial place of Wyman Johnson was found. Francis Bacon, the patriotic instructor of the Seneca County GAR, received word from the quartermaster general of the U.S. Army that the grave of Wyman J. Johnson had been found in the Confederate cemetery, where a tombstone had been erected to his memory.

THE BEGINNING OF THE FAME OF THE SCYTHE TREE

Shortly after the initial Memorial Day celebrations in 1866 in Waterloo, Lucinda Jane McCurdy Bone, a neighbor of the Johnsons, held a private memorial in Wyman's honor. She and her friend Seth Genung left evergreen wreaths and bouquets of flowers at the base of the Scythe Tree.[144] In those many years following Wyman's death, the tree grew to maturity, measuring one hundred feet in height and over five feet in diameter. The scythe became imbedded in the very heart of the tree, with only a few inches of the blade protruding. The wooden handle of the scythe decayed and dropped off. In 1916, a bolt of lightning struck the tree, rendering the bark from top to bottom and killing three of its limbs but not injuring the scythe. The tree was then treated and survived.[145] As Mildred Morgan described it so well, "No memorial can match the living one that breathes on the Johnson farm."[146] For many years, the Women's Relief Corps of the Tyler J. Snyder Post No. 72, GAR, placed a new flag on this historic tree whenever it was needed.

THE SCHAFFER BROTHERS AND WORLD WAR I

The onset of American involvement in World War I led to another major chapter in this story. Two young men living on the Scythe Tree Farm, as it was by then commonly known, enlisted. They were the sons of Mr. C.L. Schaffer, who owned the farm at the time. Raymond L. Schaffer enlisted in the U.S. Army on January 18, 1918, and was called into service in Company F, Thirty-third Engineers, at Camp Devens, Massachusetts, on March 22, 1918. On leaving his home, he placed his scythe in the tree. The carpenter's local union, No. 187 of Geneva, of which he was a member, kept an American flag floating over his scythe. On May 28, 1918, his only and younger brother, Lynn E. Schaffer, enlisted in the U.S. Navy at Geneva and was called into service on May 29, 1918, at the Naval Training Station in Great Lakes, Illinois. He, too, hung a scythe beside his brother's. The Young Men's Bible Class of the First Presbyterian Church of Waterloo, of which he was a member, kept the American flag flying over his scythe. This meant that a total of three American flags were kept continually waving over the three scythes until the close of World War I—one each in honor of James Wyman Johnson, Raymond Schaffer and Lynn Schaffer.

The two Schaffer boys safely returned home, and each removed the handle from his scythe, leaving the blade in the tree.[147] Their two flags were taken down.

This second poem about the Scythe Tree is taken from the November 15, 1933 issue of *Finger Lakes Topics* and is written by Frances Crosby Hamlet:

A stalwart lad in the burning sun,
That anxious summer of '61,
Young Johnson toiled on the farm alone,
Tilling the crops his father had sown.

Bull Run was fought. That father had said,
"The lad's too young; I must go instead."
With a wistful smile and a wave of the arm,
He turned his back on his pleasant farm.

Weeding, harvesting, making hay,
Tending the "critters" from day to day,
The boy's thoughts clung round that struggle grim.
Young? But Lincoln had need for him.

The last crops garnered, impetuously
He hung his scythe in a dooryard tree;
"I'm off, dear mother; don't worry a bit,
Just leave my scythe till I come for it!"

The father came. But the boy's scythe clung
Just where its shining blade was flung.
The grim war ended, its lessons learned;
But no laughing lad to that scythe returned.

He never came; still that dooryard tree
Guards its rusty blade—and a memory.
And the town still speaks of that soldier son
Who farmed and fought in '61.[148]

THE CONTINUING FAME OF THE SCYTHE TREE

Sometime after the flags in honor of the Schaffer brothers were removed, the Waterloo Rotary Club erected a modest granite marker near the tree, giving the pertinent facts of its story. Today, one can see only the tips of the blades of all three scythes hanging in the tree. Each blade tip has been painted to make them easier to spot.

Though time has passed and the aged tree continues to deteriorate, its fame lives on. In July 1990, the New York State Department of Environmental Conservation named the Scythe Tree as one of eleven trees to be of "extraordinary historic significance."[149] The Scythe Tree is listed by the National Arbor Day Foundation as one of the "Majestic Trees of America."[150]

In September 2002, Faye Sizemore published this poem in tribute to the history and meaning of the tree:

Waterloo's Women's Relief Corps at the Scythe Tree on Memorial Day, 1927. *Waterloo Historical Society.*

The Scythe Tree

A farmer boy did answer the call to war
He hung his scythe in a cottonwood tree;
Little did he know he'd not need it any more.
Around it for years the tree did grow
It cradled his scythe just so
A monument to a brave Union soldier
Who never came home and this is why
He was captured and so did die
in South Carolina in a confederate infirmary
His scythe in New York still remains in the tree
though only the tip of it you now can see
a salute to brave James W. Johnson
who fought for all people to be free
And this soldier was not to be the last one
Years later World War One was raging on
Alongside James's the boys also hung their scythes
And to fight in a foreign land they were gone
The tree still stands through the summers and ice
A living tribute to brave soldiers gone to war;
May it stand in remembrance forevermore.[151]

CONTINUED MAINTENANCE OF THE AGING TREE

Recently, the condition of the tree has been of extreme concern. The tree suffered some damage in the ice storm of early 2003. The obvious need for repairs to the tree to restore its visual appearance, as well as the very continued existence of the old tree, prompted Sheila Agrasto, the owner of the property at that time, to approach the Town of Waterloo to fund the effort. Research into the matter made clear that the Town of Waterloo was not responsible for upkeep of the tree—the deed to the property contains a provision that the GAR had this responsibility. The Town of Waterloo did provide $300 so that the Quality Tree Service, working with the Caywood Camp, Sons of Union Veterans, could remove the branches damaged from the ice storm.[152] The Department of New

York Sons of Union Veterans chapter has spearheaded the establishment of a $500 fund for future maintenance of the tree.[153] The Sons of Union Veterans organization has replaced the GAR in its efforts to preserve the well-being of this aging tree.

The Scythe Tree remains a visual reminder of the sacrifice that many young men have made—the sacrifice of going off to war and, in many cases, not returning alive. The spirit of Wyman Johnson and the Scythe tree is well expressed in these words of the sixteen-year-old Louise Menzer: "Thus, we see this great hero of 1861 has not only a marble shaft at his last resting place, but has also a nobler monument…to mark the memory of him who sacrificed his home, his loved ones, and his life for his country."[154]

Chapter 14
CIVIL WAR MONUMENTS AND MEMORIALS IN SENECA COUNTY

There are five known Civil War monuments and/or memorials in Seneca County communities. The oldest one is in the Traver Cemetery in the town of Tyre. The newest and largest is the American Civil War Memorial in Waterloo. The other three Civil War monuments are in Seneca Falls, Lodi and Interlaken. Each pays honor and appreciation in a different way. In addition, there is a Civil War veterans section in the cemetery of deceased patients of the former Willard State Hospital for the Insane.

Soldiers' Monument in Tyre

The oldest Civil War monument in Seneca County is the Soldiers' Monument in the Traver Cemetery in the town of Tyre. Erected soon after the Civil War, this monument is the tallest gravestone in the small cemetery. Inscribed on the obelisk are the names and years of approximately twenty Tyre men who died in service during the Civil War.[155]

Soldiers and Sailors Monument in Seneca Falls

The stately Soldiers and Sailors Monument in the public park in Seneca Falls was a gift of Albert Cook. Albert Cook married Caroline Partridge, the eldest daughter of Erastus Partridge, who was engaged in the mercantile trade in Seneca Falls. Cook became president of the First National Bank of Seneca Falls in 1876. In 1880, this bank closed, and its banking business continued as the Partridge Banking House until Cook's death in October 1885. As his health was rapidly declining prior to his death, Cook expressed his desire to have a portion of his estate devoted to the erection of this monument. His widow and daughter carried out his wishes. The monument is described in a 1904 book as the "stately and beautiful soldiers and sailors monument that adorns the public park of Seneca Falls, which is the pride of the citizens of the village." It has large sculptures of a Civil War soldier and a sailor. The monument is officially known as the Albert Cook Memorial and is a memorial "to the martyrs who fell and the heroes who fought in defense of liberty and the Union, 1861–1865." Also inscribed on the monument are the phrases "Liberty and Union: Now and Forever, One and Inseparable";

The Albert Cook Memorial is also known as the Soldiers and Sailors Monument in Seneca Falls. It is the tallest Civil War monument in Seneca County. *Walter Gable.*

"The Union It Must Be Preserved"; and "That Government of the People, by the People, and for the People, shall not perish from the earth."[156]

SOLDIERS' MONUMENT IN LODI

The Soldiers' Monument in the West Lodi Cemetery was unveiled on Saturday, September 20, 1884. The unveiling ceremony took place in Gulick Grove under the direction of the Chestnut Post of the GAR, assisted by GAR posts in neighboring towns. The main address was given by DeWitt C. Bouton, Esquire, of Ithaca. William H. Chestnut of Ovid presented a banner. The banner and a copy of the dedication program are in the possession of the Lodi Historical Society. The main feature of the monument is one soldier standing, making for a stately grandeur.[157]

The Soldiers' Monument in the West Lodi Cemetery consists of one standing soldier. *Carolyn Zogg.*

A close-up of the Soldiers' Monument in the West Lodi Cemetery. *Carolyn Zogg.*

War of the Rebellion Monument in Interlaken

The War of the Rebellion Monument in Lake View Cemetery in Interlaken is quite different in appearance from the two discussed above. It does not have any soldier statue and is not as tall; rather, it has a stately simplicity with the message: "Erected to the memory of my comrades in arms of the War of the Rebellion by Madison Covert, a member of Company C, 126th Regiment, New York Volunteers." Madison Covert enlisted on August 8, 1862, at the age of twenty-four. He was severely wounded in the foot at Gettysburg on July 4, 1863, and was discharged on December 25, 1864. He was born in Lodi in 1836, the son of Isaac V. and Rachel Covert.[158]

War of the Rebellion Monument in the Lake View Cemetery in Interlaken. *Walter Gable.*

THE AMERICAN CIVIL WAR MEMORIAL IN WATERLOO

Ironically, until 2008, there was no official Civil War memorial in Waterloo. A group headed by Caren Cleaveland decided to erect a memorial in Waterloo that would honor and pay tribute to both the Union and Confederate soldiers and sailors lost during America's bloodiest war. In 2006, the group approved Pietro del Fabor's design for the American Civil War Memorial.

The American Civil War Memorial, dedicated on September 20, 2008, is located on Lock Island, Route 96 South at the Cayuga-Seneca Canal. The memorial commemorates the sacrifice made by citizens of Waterloo during the Civil War. A total of fifty-eight soldiers from Waterloo died in the Civil War; they have become known as the "Waterloo Fallen." At the time of their deaths, the men ranged in age from eighteen to forty-seven. Each of these Waterloo Fallen is remembered with a cenotaph made of Indian silver buff limestone and a brass plaque. Extensive research was done to write biographies on each deceased soldier.

View from Washington Street of the American Civil War Memorial cenotaph field. *Pietro del Fabro.*

Portal and portal wall detail of the American Civil War Memorial. *Pietro del Fabro.*

The central feature of the memorial is a marble star set in a cedar-lined enclosure with a stone portal. During the summers of 2007 and 2008, Waterloo residents worked together carving the limestone cenotaphs and the stars on the marble star. There are 620 stars, each gilded with twenty-three-carat gold and representing one thousand Union and Confederate lives lost in the conflict.

The North South Cenotaph celebrates the binding together of the thirty-six states separated during the Civil War and memorializes all lives lost during the conflict. This cenotaph is constructed of stones and bricks sent from each of these thirty-six states. Each stone and brick came with its own story, which can be read on the memorial website: www.americancivilwarmemorial.com.

A Women's Cenotaph commemorates the many women who served during the war in a variety of roles including doctors, spies, nurses and sometimes even soldiers. There is a Unit Cenotaph that lists the regiments in which the men of Waterloo and Seneca County served and the battles in which they fought. The memorial also has a flagpole for the U.S. flag of 1865.

Left: Sculpting the cenotaphs for the Waterloo Fallen, August 2007. *Maria del Fabro*.

Below: The North South Cenotaph of the American Civil War Memorial is constructed of stones and bricks contributed by thirty-six states. *Pietro del Fabro*.

The Daughters of Union Veterans of the Civil War, 1861–1865, New York Department, took ownership of the memorial on August 25, 2009. The group is active in all the affairs of the memorial, including arranging ceremonies at the site, giving tours and coordinating events with reenactor units and government and historical organizations.

Research on the Waterloo Fallen continues. Many Civil War soldiers who died in combat were buried in unmarked graves. Initial research had located the actual gravesites of only eighteen of the fifty-eight Waterloo Fallen. Between 2010 and 2014, the graves of six more had been located.[159]

CIVIL WAR VETERANS BURIED IN THE WILLARD STATE HOSPITAL CEMETERY

Over 150 patients of the Willard Asylum for the Insane (renamed the Willard State Hospital in 1890) are buried in a section of the cemetery of the facility. Nearly 6,000 Willard hospital patients died between 1870 and 2000 and were buried in the hospital cemetery when the body was not claimed by family members.[160] The Civil War veterans section of the cemetery is located in the northwestern portion of the cemetery, nearest to Seneca Lake. There is a grave marker for each of the veterans buried in this section. Almost all of these grave markers are of stone and identify basic information about the person's Civil War service. Just a handful of the markers are wooden. Significantly, there are very few gravestones in the rest of the cemetery.[161]

Some of the Civil War veterans buried in this cemetery came from the immediate Seneca County area, but most came from other parts of New York State. They served in the various regiments of the Union forces, both army and navy. Some were deserters. Some were held as prisoners during a portion of the Civil War. Some received pensions.

For most of these veterans, little is known except for their war service information and the date of burial at the hospital cemetery. For a few of the soldiers, however, former Seneca County Historian Betty Auten was able to uncover some information. William Collins, for example, was a member of the party that helped capture John Wilkes Booth, the assassin of President Abraham Lincoln. Collins received a special pension for his efforts. He had lived in Albion prior to his military service. He died on March 25, 1904.[162]

Chapter 15

GAR POSTS AND AFFILIATED AND SUCCESSOR ORGANIZATIONS IN SENECA COUNTY

History and Structure of the Grand Army of the Republic

The Grand Army of the Republic (GAR) was founded in Decatur, Illinois, on April 6, 1866, by Benjamin F. Stephenson. The organization was based on the three cardinal principles of fraternity, charity and loyalty. Membership was limited to honorably discharged veterans of the Union army, navy, marine corps or revenue cutter service who had served between April 12, 1861, and April 9, 1865. Each state or region of the GAR was called a "department," and each local unit was called a "post." Each post was numbered consecutively within its department. Most posts also had a name that honored a deceased person. The official body of the department was the annual encampment. Encampments were elaborate multi-day events, typically including camping out, formal dinners and memorial events.

The GAR founded soldiers' homes and was active in relief work and pension legislation. The political power of the GAR grew during the latter part of the nineteenth century, when it helped elect six Republican GAR members to the presidency, beginning with U.S. Grant and ending with William McKinley.[163] In 1888, President Grover Cleveland, a Democrat, vetoed a bill to grant pensions to veterans' dependents. President Cleveland was defeated in his run for a second term in November 1888. In 1890, with

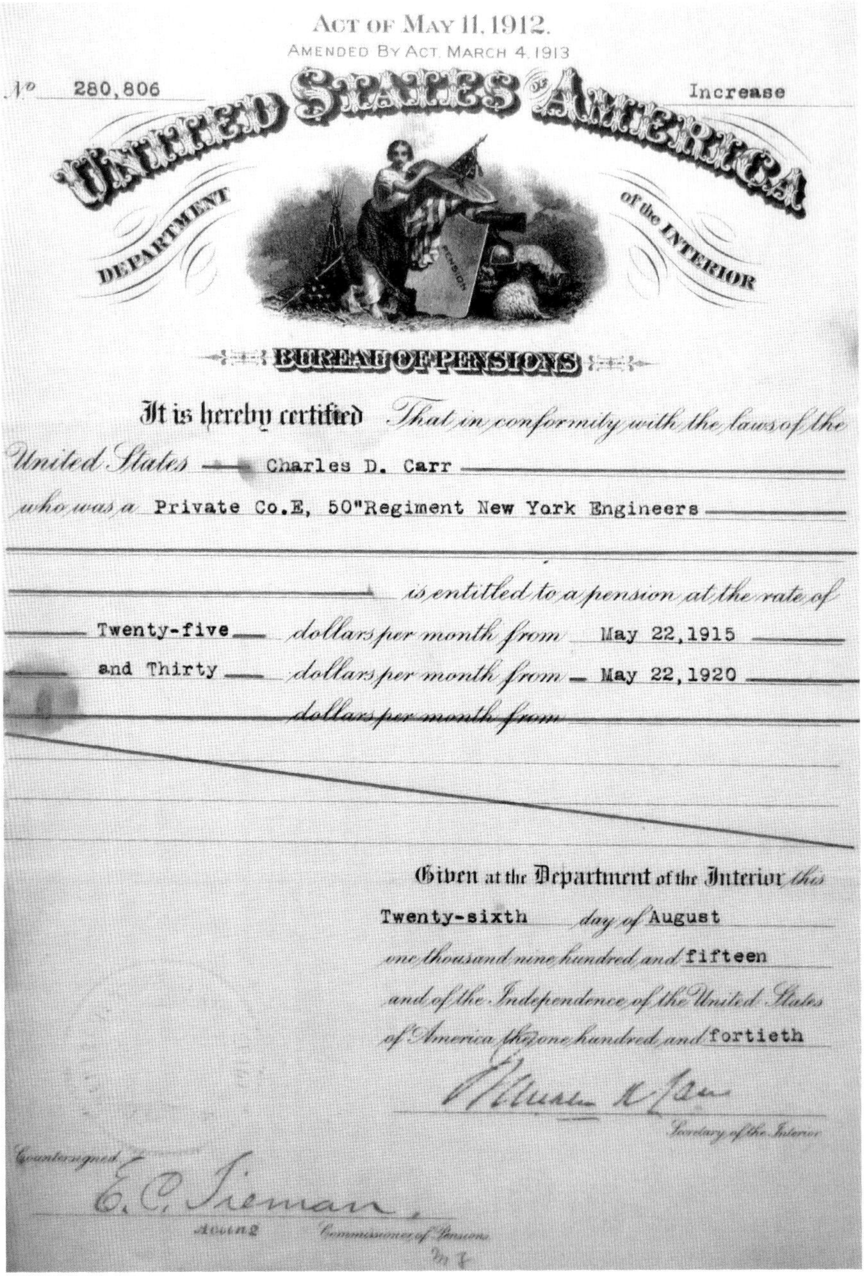

Act of May 11, 1912.
Amended By Act. March 4, 1913

No 280,806 Increase

United States of America

Department of the Interior

Pension

Bureau of Pensions

It is hereby certified That in conformity with the laws of the United States Charles D. Carr who was a Private Co.E, 50"Regiment New York Engineers is entitled to a pension at the rate of Twenty-five dollars per month from May 22,1915 and Thirty dollars per month from May 22,1920 dollars per month from

Given at the Department of the Interior this Twenty-sixth day of August one thousand nine hundred and fifteen and of the Independence of the United States of America the one hundred and fortieth

Secretary of the Interior

Countersigned, E. C. Tieman, Acting Commissioner of Pensions

1915 pension record of Charles D. Carr showing he was entitled to $25 a month for the next 5 years and then $30 a month starting in 1920. *Waterloo Historical Society*.

Uniform of a GAR member. *Waterloo Historical Society*.

Ribbons of various GAR members and reunions. *Waterloo Historical Society.*

the support of President Benjamin Harrison, who had been supported by the GAR, the Disability Pension Act was passed, granting pensions to any disabled veteran who had served at least ninety days.[164]

The final encampment of the Grand Army of the Republic was held in Indianapolis, Indiana, in 1949, with six GAR members in attendance.

The last member of the GAR was Albert Woolson, who died in 1956 at the age of 109.

With membership limited strictly to "veterans of the late unpleasantness," the GAR encouraged the formation of Allied Orders to help in various works. Some of the Allied Orders were the Sons of Veterans of the United States of America, the Women's Relief Corps, the Ladies of the Grand Army of the Republic and the Daughters of Union Veterans of the Civil War.

General John A. Logan became the national commander-in-chief in 1867. He is best remembered as the man who issued General Order No. 11 in 1868, which instructed each GAR post to have a Memorial Day event on May 30 of that year and each year thereafter.

The GAR almost disappeared as a national organization in the early 1870s when many departments ceased to exist. New leadership emerged in 1875 with a platform of renewed growth. The GAR reached its largest membership in 1890 with nearly 500,000 members.[165]

HONORING THE GAR ON DECORATION DAY IN 1874

On Decoration Day 1874, the Honorable Albert L. Childs of Waterloo read one of his original poems at a meeting held at Steinway Hall in New York City. Henry Ward Beecher, the great abolitionist preacher, delivered the oration at that meeting. Miss Clara Louis Kellogg, a celebrated soloist, sang patriotic songs. The last verse of Childs's poem is as follows:

Grand Army of Republic! Always grand!
On us thy valor hath an endless claim;
When Freedom's foes would desolate the land,
Thy presence saved our banner from the shame!
Grand Army of Republic! Always grand!
With thee our stars shall never fade away;
God bless our living soldiers as they stand
Around our dead this Decoration Day![166]

A 1931 picture of the last four surviving Civil War veterans from Waterloo: Jacob Sands, George K. Marshall, John Hill and Peter Cadmus. *Waterloo Historical Society.*

TYLER J. SNYDER POST NO. 72 IN WATERLOO

The GAR post in Waterloo was named in memory of Tyler J. Snyder. Snyder had enlisted in Company G of the 126th New York Infantry on August 14, 1862, at the age of twenty-one. He was shot in the leg at Gettysburg on July 2, 1863, and died in the field hospital. He is buried in the National Cemetery at Gettysburg.[167]

For many years, the Tyler Post was housed on the third floor of the Brooks & Manning's brick block, located on the south side of West Main Street in Waterloo.[168]

The Tyler J. Snyder Post No. 78 Women's Relief Corps was organized on April 13, 1886, with sixteen charter members. Mrs. Elizabeth Lerch was the president, Mrs. Carrie Sand was senior vice-president, Mrs. Mary Feighty was junior vice-president, Mrs. Maggie Donnalley was secretary and Miss Kate Hull was treasurer. This society was of great support to the GAR and the village in general. It continued to operate even after the death of the last GAR member but finally disbanded in May 1948.[169]

A gathering of the Waterloo Women's Relief Corps at the Scythe Tree. *Waterloo Historical Society*.

The last seven surviving Waterloo veterans of the Civil War. *Waterloo Historical Society*.

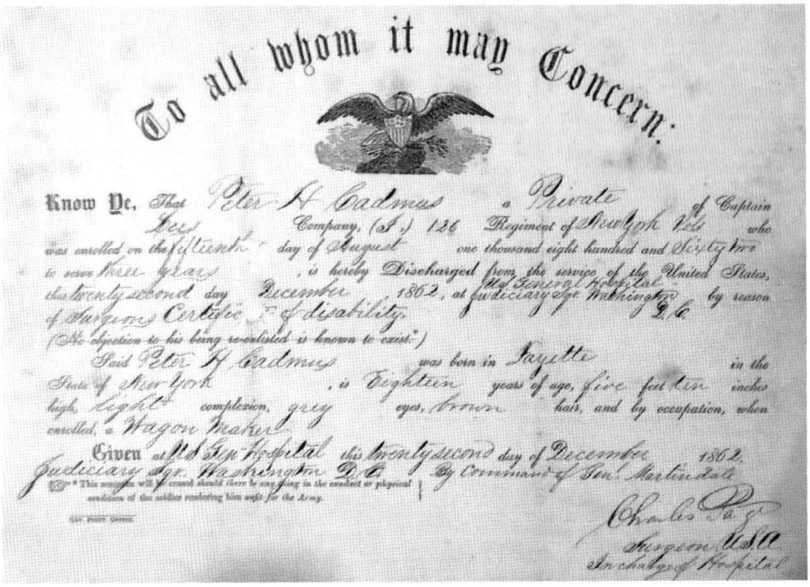

To all whom it may Concern:

Know Ye, That Peter H Cadmus a Private of Captain Lee's Company, (I.) 126 Regiment of New York Vols who was enrolled on the fifteenth day of August one thousand eight hundred and Sixty two to serve three years, is hereby Discharged from the service of the United States, this twenty second day December 1862, at U.S. General Hospital Judiciary Sqr Washington D.C. by reason of Surgeons Certificate of disability.

(No objection to his being reenlisted is known to exist.*)

Said Peter H Cadmus was born in Fayette in the State of New York, is Eighteen years of age, five feet ten inches high, light complexion, grey eyes, brown hair, and by occupation, when enrolled, a Wagon Maker.

Given at U.S. Genl Hospital Judiciary Sqr. Washington D.C. this twenty second day of December 1862. By Command of Genl. Martindale

*This sentence will be erased should there be anything in the conduct or physical condition of the soldier rendering him unfit for the Army.

Charles Page
Surgeon USA
In charge of Hospital

The December 22, 1862 discharge papers of Peter H. Cadmus. *Waterloo Historical Society*.

The last three Waterloo surviving Civil War veterans were John Hill, Peter Cadmus and Jacob Sands. *Waterloo Historical Society*.

The thinning in the ranks of living Civil War veterans who were members of the Tyler post was quite obvious in the 1920 Memorial Day parade. Only thirteen members of the post marched in the parade. One automobile transported veterans unable to march. The graves of four hundred deceased comrades were decorated with flowers. The post had twenty members at that time, only half of them able to attend meetings.[170]

In August 1932, there were only four surviving members of this GAR post: John M. Hill, Peter H. Cadmus, George K. Marshall and Jacob Sands.[171] On February 10, 1934, the three surviving members—Cadmus, Hill and Sands—were photographed on the entrance porch of the Waterloo Library and Historical Society.[172]

SONS OF VETERANS POSTS IN WATERLOO

On January 24, 1887, the George Donnalley Post No. 59, Sons of Veterans, was organized. George G. Donnalley was the commander; Henry Fairchild, senior vice-commander; Sidney M. Smith, junior vice-commander; James Colligan, adjutant; William Ackerman, quartermaster; Fred G. Cox, surgeon; Frank Smith, chaplain; Edward Richardson, officer of the day; George Gilbert, inside sentinel; and William Tewksbury, outside sentinel. This post disbanded in a short period of time.

On July 17, 1890, the William G. Cook Camp 59, Sons of Veterans, was organized.[173] There was also the John B. Murray Command, Union Veterans Union, which elected the following officers in December 1894: George Dilts, colonel; Abram Schott, lieutenant colonel; Jacob Sands, major; James Clark, chaplain; George Hogoboom, quartermaster; John Morrin, officer of the day; and Frank Lamphere, officer of the guard.[174]

ANDREW J. CHESTNUT POST NO. 445, GAR, IN LODI

The Lodi GAR Post No. 445 was formed on January 28, 1884. It is named in memory of Andrew J. Chestnut. Charter members were David Armstrong, E.C. Baker, James M. Bennett, James D. Brown, Lewis P. Brown, J.L. Bodine,

Joseph Burdin, William B. Clawson, Elisha Covert, H.C. Gardner, James A. Huff, William H. Jackson, J. MaGee, M. McEvoy, David P. Miller, John C. Parker, Henry Peterson, D.H. Predmore, D. Spencer, J.H. Stevens, Benjamin Swarthout, N.O. Swarthout, Oliver Slaght, Isaac H. Stevens, B.J. Tracy, A.V. Tunison and J.F. Van Vleet.[175]

At the age of twenty-three, Andrew J. Chestnut enlisted on August 8, 1862, in Company C of the 126th New York Infantry. Having emigrated from Ireland, he was a farmer at the time of his enlistment. He was killed at Morton's Ford, Virginia, on February 6, 1864. He is buried in the West Lodi Cemetery, where his tombstone bears the following epitaph: "Angels bear him safely upward; Place his head on Jesus' breast; From the field of battle bear him; Up where all is peace and rest."[176]

WILLIAM E. AVERY POST NO. 438, GAR, IN INTERLAKEN

The William E. Avery Post No. 438, GAR, was organized at Farmer Village on December 29, 1883, with eighty-five members. It was named in memory of Lieutenant William E. Avery.

Interlaken Civil War veterans gathered in the Lake View Cemetery in Interlaken, 1910. *Interlaken Historical Society*.

Born in the town of Covert, twenty-three-year-old William Avery enlisted on September 18, 1861, in Company F of the Seventy-fifth New York Infantry. He was killed on May 27, 1863, in the charge at Port Hudson, Louisiana. He is buried in the Lake View Cemetery in Interlaken.

In addition to organizing and participating in various annual memorial festivities, the post was active in providing relief to sick and disabled veterans, facilitating the burial of deceased veterans and the erection of suitable tombstones over their graves and other charitable acts. Post member Madison Covert, who had served in Company C of the 126th New York Volunteers, donated the funds to erect a memorial known as the War of the Rebellion Monument in Lake View Cemetery. The post continued until the death of John R. Ryno in 1930.[177]

GAR Posts in Ovid

The Charles P. Little Post No. 40, GAR, in Ovid was established on October 3, 1874.[178] The original charter member officers were Henry V.L. Jones, commander; Henry Peterson, senior vice-commander; Archibald M. Covert, junior vice-commander; Lewis D. Woodruff, adjutant; Francis M. Rappleye, officer of the day; James M. Conover, officer of the guard; Abram Wilson, chaplain; Patrick Carroll, quartermaster; John A.L. Bodine, quartermaster-sergeant; and Alton Van Horn, sergeant-major. During the first two and a half years of its existence, this post expended several hundred dollars in fitting up a soldiers' lot in the Union Cemetery for the burial of poor soldiers who served in the war, depositing therein the bodies of those already deceased and buried in Potter's Field and placing suitable headstones over their graves. It also provided relief to its sick and disabled comrades and performed other charitable acts, meriting the just praise of a grateful and appreciating community. The post's largest membership was fifty-six. Down to twenty-one members in 1876, the Little Post was soon disbanded.

On December 30, 1880, a charter was granted to the Charles T. Harris Post No. 325, Department of New York, at a meeting convened in the county courthouse in Ovid. John W. Swarthout was elected its first commander. The Harris Post met on alternate Fridays in the Independent Order of Good Templars (IOGT) Hall.[179]

CROSS POST NO. 78, GAR, IN SENECA FALLS

The Cross Post No. 78, GAR, in Seneca Falls is named in honor of William Cross and five of his sons, all of whom served in the Civil War. This Cross Post is the oldest of the county's GAR posts, having been established in 1868. The charter members were Chas. J. Martin, Geo. B. Davis, E. Golder, Wm. Failing, W.H. Golder, Richard Golder, Lorenzo Baker, Edward Rinker, Alex Davit, Geo. Speer, John Morris, Elias Lester and H.V. Matthews. The post had a membership of nearly 300 in 1868.[180] That number was down to 120 in 1875.

All of this post's records, flags, pictures and mementoes of the Civil War, together with its furniture, were totally destroyed in the great village fire of July 30, 1890. This following description of the post was made in a 1905 publication:

> *The present members of Cross Post are the survivors of a host that went out from home and friends to fight the battles for the existence of the Union in such numbers as to make Seneca Falls the banner town, by furnishing a larger percentage of its people for soldiers and sailors for that war than any other township in our state. No battle was fought on sea or land during those four years but had its Seneca Falls representative. There was no profession or trade that was distinctly drawn upon—all were equally patriotic.*[181]

Cross Corps No. 10 of the Women's Relief Corps was founded in 1884 as an auxiliary to the Cross Post. Charter members were Imogene L. Guion, Virginia N. Havens, Jennie P. Shepard, Emma Ruthrauff, Ruth Perry, Nellie Sherman, Jennie Timmerman, Elizabeth Adams, Celia B. Randolph, Libbie T. Demorest, Susan E. Travor, Jennie C. McDuffe, Hannah E. Waldo, Vashti E. Smith, Frederica Brown, Cornelia Fegley and Helen Girioux. The Cross Corps had sixty-two members in 1904. Two of their major long-term projects have been placing flags in public schools and providing relief to aged and dependent wives or mothers of veterans.[182]

SONS OF UNION VETERANS OF THE CIVIL WAR

The present-day Sons of Union Veterans of the Civil War is an outgrowth of the Corps of Cadets created by the Grand Army of the Republic in 1878. On November 12, 1881, the Corps of Cadets became the Sons of Veterans of the United States of America (SV). The SV units functioned much like National Guard units and actually served along with state militia during the Spanish-American War.

In 1904, the SV elected to become a patriotic education society. In 1925, the SV changed its name to Sons of Union Veterans of the Civil War (SUVCW). It kept within its organization the Sons of Veterans Reserve (SVR), which was carried on the army rolls as a reserve contingent. Some SVR units served with the army during World War I.

In more recent years, the SVR's mission has become historic, ceremonial and commemorative. Prior to its disbandment, the GAR

The "Baby Bear" building (the smallest of the three former county government buildings) housed the Ovid GAR post for many years and currently houses the Caywood Camp, Sons of Union Veterans. *Walter Gable.*

Logo for the Caywood Camp, Sons of Union Veterans, on the door of the Baby Bear building. *Walter Gable.*

officially designated the SUVCW as the successor and heir to its remaining property. On August 20, 1954, Congress enacted Public Law 605, officially incorporating the SUVCW.[183]

The Caywood Camp, New York Department of the SUVCW, was chartered in January 1914. The Caywood Camp has been housed in the "Baby Bear," the smallest of the three Seneca County government buildings in Ovid. Prior to the Sons of Union Veterans camp, the Baby Bear had been the meeting place of the Ovid GAR post. The Caywood Camp members are active in participating in many local events, such as Salute the Troops at Sampson State Park each August and the Celebrate Commemorate events in Waterloo each Memorial Day weekend. Caywood Camp members also attend regional and state meetings and events. The Caywood Camp has an affiliated David G. Caywood Camp Auxiliary #72 that is also active. It currently has about thirty members.[184]

DAUGHTERS OF UNION VETERANS OF THE CIVIL WAR

The Daughters of Union Veterans of the Civil War, 1861–1865, (DUVCW) is an outgrowth of the National Alliance Daughters of Veterans that was organized on May 30, 1885. The National Alliance Daughters of Veterans was endorsed by the GAR in 1900. The name of the organization was changed to Daughters of Union Veterans of the Civil War in 1925. In 1944, the name was changed to Daughters of Union Veterans of the Civil War, 1861–1865. A federal charter was granted by Public Law 99-1972 on December 9, 1985.[185]

The DUVCW consists of direct-line female descendants from honorably discharged veterans of the Union army and navy who fought in the defense and for the preservation of the United States during the American Civil War. The group honors Union veterans through service projects that are of benefit to the public at the local, state and national levels. This national organization has local groups, known as "tents." These tents are named for army nurses who served in the Civil War or any loyal woman of the Civil War era whose patriotic deeds during the years 1861-1865 were recorded. The New York Department, DUVCW, was organized on July 27, 1893, and has six active tents.[186] The Mary Gahan Tent, located in Waterloo, was dedicated on May 29, 2010. The tent has assumed responsibilities for the maintenance of the American Civil War Memorial (ACWM) in Waterloo. Members of the Mary Gahan Tent plan various events at the ACWM throughout the year, but especially as part of the Celebrate Commemorate events of Memorial Day weekend.[187]

NOTES

1. "The Impending Revolution," a January 5, 1861 article appearing in a Seneca County newspaper, probably the *Seneca County Courier*.
2. Information taken from various newspaper articles assembled by Seneca Falls village historian Roberta Halden and accessible at the Seneca Falls Library.
3. Alfred H. Guernsey and Henry M. Alden, *Harper's Pictorial History of the Civil War* Volume I (Chicago: Star Publishing Company, 1868), 112.
4. Information taken from various newspaper articles assembled by Seneca Falls village historian Roberta Halden and accessible at the Seneca Falls Library.
5. Ibid.
6. Ibid.
7. John E. Becker, *A History of the Village of Waterloo, New York and Thesaurus of Related Facts* (Waterloo, NY: Waterloo Library and Historical Society, 1949), 171–72.
8. www.dmna.ny.gov/historic/reghist/civil/infantry/33rdInf/33rdInfMain.htm.
9. H.F. Brehm, former historian for the Waterloo Library and Historical Society.
10. George W. Contant, *Path of Blood: The True Story of the 33rd New York Volunteers* (Savannah, NY: Seeco Printing Services, 1996).
11. Information taken from the notebooks of newspaper clippings in the Seneca Falls Library.
12. Ibid.

13. *Geneva Gazette* and *Geneva Courier* newspaper articles at the Geneva Historical Society.
14. *Finger Lakes Times*, July 11, 1987.
15. *Finger Lakes Times*, June 26, 1978.
16. *Geneva Courier*, August 13, 1862.
17. *Penn Yan Democrat*, September 4, 1914.
18. *Finger Lakes Times*, July 11, 1987.
19. Wayne Mahood, *Written in Blood: A History of the 126th New York Infantry in the Civil War* (Hightstown, NJ: Longstreet House, 1997), 8–9.
20. http://dmna.ny.gov/historic.reghist/civil/infantry/126thInf/12thInfMain.htm.
21. Mahood, *Written in Blood*, 18–20.
22. http://dmna.ny.gov/historic.reghist/civil/infantry/126thInf/12thInfMain.htm.
23. Ibid.
24. http://www.gettysburg.stonesentinels.com/NY/126NY.php.
25. Wayne E. Morrison Sr., *History of Covert, Seneca Co., N.Y.* (Ovid, NY: Wayne E. Morrison Sr., 1983), 51.
26. Betty Auten, "Civil War Soldiers of Seneca County, New York," unpublished manuscript.
27. Morrison, *History of Covert*, 51.
28. Information taken from a newspaper article in the National Memorial Day Museum.
29. Information taken from genealogical index cards prepared by former Seneca County Historian Betty Auten.
30. Auten, "Civil War Soldiers of Seneca County."
31. www.dmna.ny.gov/historic/reghist/civil/infantry/148thInf/148thInfMain.htm.
32. R.L. Murray, *Seneca County Troops in the Civil War: Letters from the Front* (Wolcott, NY: Benedum Books, 2005).
33. Information taken from the notebooks of newspaper clippings in the Seneca Falls Library.
34. http://dmna.ny.gov/historic/reghist/civil/infantry/148thInf/148thInfMain.htm.
35. http://genealogytrails.com/ny/medalofhonor_civilwar.html.
36. *History of Seneca County, New York* (Philadelphia: Everts, Ensign & Everts, 1876), 58.
37. Civilwarintheeast.com/USA/NY/NY019.php (Note: The Everts *History of Seneca County* on page 58 gives this date of organization as May 14, 1861.)
38. *History of Seneca County*, 58.
39. www.civilwarintheeast.com.
40. *History of Seneca County*, 58.
41. http://dmna.ny.gov/historic/reghist/civil/artillery/3rdArtLight/3rdArtLtMain.htm.

42. http://dmna.ny.gov/historic/reghist/civil/other/15thEng/15thEngMain.htm.
43. http://ranger95.com/civil_war_us/new_york/engineers/15th_ny_engineers.htm.
44. http://dmna.ny.gov/historic/reghist/civil/other/15thEng/15thEngMain.htm.
45. *History of Seneca County*, 59.
46. Ibid.
47. www.nps.gov/civilwar/search-regiments-detail.htm?regiment_id=UNY0015RE02.
48. http://dmna.ny.gov/historic/reghist/civil/infantry/44thInf/44thInfHistSketch.htm.
49. www.bluegrayreview.com/2012/07/24/a-banner-day/.
50. www.americancivilwarmemorial.com.
51. https://dmna.ny.gov/historic/reghist/civil/other/50thEng/50thEngMain.htm.
52. *History of Seneca County*, 63.
53. www.nps.gov/civilwar/search-regiments-detail.htm?regiment_id=UNY0050RE.
54. https://dmna.ny.gov/historic/reghist/civil/other/50thEng/50thEngMain.htm.
55. *History of Seneca County*, 64.
56. www.bluegrayreview.com/2013/03/28/present-arms.
57. https://dmna.ny.gov/historic/reghist/civil/infaantry/75thInf/75thInfMain.htm.
58. *History of Seneca County*, 66.
59. www.civilwarintheeast.com/USA/NY/NY075.php.
60. https://dmna.ny.gov/historic/reghist/civil/infaantry/75thInf/75thInfMain.htm.
61. http://www.cmohs.org/medal-history.php.
62. http://en.wikipedia.org/wiki/Medal_of_Honor.
63. http://www.homeofheroes.com/moh/history/history_statistics.html.
64. http://dmna.ny.gov.historic/reseearch/MOH/MOH_index.htm.
65. Contant, *Path of Blood*, 364.
66. *Rochester Democrat and Chronicle*, June 2, 1915.
67. Curran to the Secretary of War, affidavit date unreadable, Curran Moll Case File.
68. Affidavit by Lieutenant Bernard Byrne, Company K, Thirty-third New York Volunteers, Richard Curran Medal of Honor Case File, R&P, No. 504,522.
69. Contant, *Path of Blood*, 364–66.
70. Chuck Agonito, "Forgotten Hero from Waterloo," *Finger Lakes Times*, September 23, 2012.
71. Auten, "Civil War Soldiers of Seneca County."
72. http://www.cumpston.org.uk.

73. http://www.findagrave.com/cgi-bin/fg.cgi?page=gr&GRid=8040613.
74. Auten, "Civil War Soldiers of Seneca County."
75. http://www.homeofheroes.com/gravesites/states/pages_af/compson_hartwell_or.html.
76. http://www.findagrave.com/cgi-bin/fg.cgi?page=gr&GRid=8040613.
77. http://www.cumpston.org.uk.
78. http://en.wikipedia.org/wiki/Hartwell_B._Compson.
79. Auten, "Civil War Soldiers of Seneca County."
80. http://en.wikipedia.org/wiki/Hartwell_B._Compson.
81. Information taken from the research of former Seneca County Historian Betty Auten (mainly from her unpublished book manuscript, "Civil War Soldiers of Seneca County, New York.")
82. *Seneca County Courier*, "Cross Post to Lose Charter," 1930.
83. George Shadman, *They Marched on Richmond: The Story of the Gallant 148th New York Volunteers* (Watkins Glen, NY: G. Shadman, 1996), 206.
84. Ibid.
85. *Phelps Advertiser*, Mary Gahan obituary, July 15, 1881.
86. Shadman, *They Marched on Richmond*, 206.
87. *Phelps Advertiser*, Mary Gahan obituary.
88. Ibid.
89. Much of the information for this section on the Blew brothers has been provided by Naomi Brewer.
90. Information supplied by Naomi Brewer; Auten, "Civil War Soldiers of Seneca County."
91. Auten, "Civil War Soldiers of Seneca County."
92. Ibid.
93. Information found in the genealogical files in the Seneca County Historian's Office and Auten, " Civil War Soldiers of Seneca County."
94. *The Record* (Fall 2013).
95. Auten, "Civil War Soldiers of Seneca County."
96. Dorothy Souhan King, "A History of the Souhan Family," unpublished manuscript, 1–2.
97. *Seneca County Courier*, "John Hill Observes 94th Natal Day—Last G.A.R. Man," 1940.
98. Information supplied by Doreen Suffredini Brown, great-granddaughter of John M. Hill.
99. *Seneca County Courier*, "John Hill Observes 94th Natal Day."
100. Stephen Light, "Love at War: The Civil War Courtship of John L. Hoster and Josephine Cole," 2008 master's thesis for the Cooperstown Graduate Program.

101. Paul G. Avery and Patrick H. Garrow, *Phase III Archaeological Investigations at 38FL2, The Florence Stockade, Florence, South Carolina* (Knoxville, TN: MACTEC Engineering and Consulting Inc., 2008).
102. Ibid., 48–49.
103. David C. Smith, "Middle Range Farming in the Civil War Era: Life on a Farm in Seneca County, 1862–1866," *New York History*, October 1967.
104. Information taken from notebooks of newspaper clippings in the Seneca Falls Library.
105. Edith Delavan, *Landmarks of Seneca County* (Ithaca, NY: Cayuga Press, 2004), 136.
106. Information taken from notebooks of newspaper clippings in the Seneca Falls Library.
107. Ibid.
108. Ibid.
109. Official elections results in the records of the Seneca County Board of Elections.
110. Information taken from notebooks of newspaper clippings in the Seneca Falls Library.
111. Official elections results in the records of the Seneca County Board of Elections.
112. Information taken from the notebooks of newspaper clippings in the Seneca Falls Library.
113. Ibid.
114. *Proceedings of the Board of Supervisors of Seneca County for the Year 1864* (Seneca Falls, NY: Reveille Book and Job Office, 1864).
115. www.usmemorialday.org/order11.html.
116. www.waterloony.com/MemDay.html.
117. www1.va.gov/opa/speceven/memday/history.asp.
118. www.womenshistory.about.com/cs/holidays/a/memorial_day.htm.
119. www.usmemorialday.org/ backgrnd.html.
120. Ibid.
121. www.waterloony.com/MemDay/html.
122. Becker, *A History of the Village of Waterloo*, 185.
123. Ibid.
124. Ibid., 187.
125. http://www.waterloony.com/MemDay.html.
126. www.nytimes.com/2012/05/27/us/many-claim-to-be-memorial-day-birthplace.html.
127. Unpublished research work of Richard Burtless of Seneca Falls.

128. www1.va.gov/opa/speceven/memday/history.asp.
129. Unpublished research work of Richard Burtless of Seneca Falls.
130. www.nytimes.com/2012/05/27/us/many-claim-to-be-memorial-day-birthplace.html.
131. http://www.wlhs-ny-.org/NationalMemorialDayMuseum.html.
132. Information supplied by Caren Cleaveland.
133. Louise Menzer, "History of the Scythe Tree," taken from War Records and prepared for the Seneca County Chamber of Commerce, 1988.
134. *The Conservationist*, "New York's Famous and Historic Trees," (March–April 1987), 32.
135. Menzer, "History of the Scythe Tree."
136. Ibid.
137. Wayne Mahood, "Until I Return: The Legend of the Scythe Tree," *Civil War Times Illustrated* 25, no. 9 (January 1987).
138. Menzer, "History of the Scythe Tree."
139. Mahood, "Until I Return."
140. There is some question as to whether the grave was "unmarked" or "unknown." Mildred Morgan, in her September 2002 story, uses the word "unmarked" to refer to the grave. It is not known from what newspaper her article was actually taken. In that same article, she states that when the remains were discovered, they were taken to a national cemetery, where a tombstone was erected as a memorial.
141. Mahood, "Until I Return."
142. Menzer, "History of the Scythe Tree."
143. *Seneca County Courier*, "Woman Who Cared for Famous Scythe Tree Buried in Maple Grove," May 2, 1930.
144. Mahood, "Until I Return."
145. Menzer, "History of the Scythe Tree."
146. Mildred Morgan, "A Soldier's Scythe," September 2002 newspaper article (actual name of newspaper not identified but likely *The Voice* newsletter for the ECC Retirement Village in Myerstown, Pennsylvania).
147. "A Soldier's Scythe Tree," Waterloo Women's Reading Club story donated by Ella Strong, March 1, 1988.
148. Becker, *A History of the Village of Waterloo*, 505–06.
149. *Rochester Democrat and Chronicle*, "Three Local Trees Among the Elite 11," September 9, 1990, B1.
150. http://arborday.org/trees/majTreesTimeline.html.
151. http://www.iwvpa.net/sizemoref/the_sc.htm.
152. Telephone conversation with Joyce Fredericks, September 3, 2003.

153. Telephone conversation with Dale E. Theetge, September 3, 2003.
154. Menzer, "History of the Scythe Tree."
155. *History of Seneca County*, 127.
156. Edgar Luderne Welch, *Grip's Historical Souvenir of Seneca Falls* (Syracuse, NY: Grip, 1904), 141–42. (Reprinted by the Seneca Falls Historical Society in 1991.)
157. Wayne E. Morrison Sr., *History of Lodi, Seneca Co., N.Y.* (Ovid, NY: W.E. Morrison & Co., n.d.), 68.
158. Morrison, *History of Covert*, 62.
159. Information supplied by Caren Cleaveland.
160. *Finger Lakes Times*, "Willard's Lost Souls," April 14, 2011.
161. William Sebring, Romulus town historian, April 21, 2014.
162. Betty Auten, "Civil War Soldiers of Seneca County."
163. www.garmuslib.org/banner.htm.
164. "The Grand Army of the Republic," *The Record* 10, no. 4 (Fall 2013).
165. www.garmuslib.org/banner.htm.
166. Becker, *A History of the Village of Waterloo*, 209.
167. Betty Auten, "Civil War Soldiers of Seneca County."
168. Becker, *A History of the Village of Waterloo*, 261.
169. Ibid., 269–70.
170. Ibid., 382.
171. Ibid., 413.
172. Ibid., 415.
173. Ibid., 273
174. Ibid., 303.
175. Morrison, *History of Lodi*, 68.
176. "The Andrew J. Chestnut Post No. 445, GAR," *The Record* 10, no. 4 (Fall 2013).
177. Morrison, *History of Covert*, 62.
178. *History of Seneca County*, 53.
179. Morrison, *History of Ovid*, 117.
180. Welch, *Grip's Historical Souvenir*, 46.
181. Ibid.
182. Ibid., 33.
183. www.suvcw.org/suv.htm.
184. Information supplied by Diane Theetge, April 17, 2014.
185. www.duvcw.org.
186. Ibid.
187. Information taken from the files in the Seneca County Historian's Office.

INDEX

ABOUT THE AUTHOR

Walter Gable has been the Seneca County Historian since August 2003. A lifelong resident of Seneca County, he is a graduate of the Romulus Central School District and earned his bachelor's and master's degrees at Syracuse University. He taught high school social studies for thirty years at Mynderse Academy in the Seneca Falls Central School District. He was president of the New York State Council for the Social Studies (1997–98) and recognized as Distinguished Social Studies Educator in New York State in 2000. He received the Seneca Falls Community Service Award in 2013. He credits his lifelong interest in history to the late Miss Ethel Buckley, his enthusiastic high school history teacher.